STEVE SOLON

MY MOTHER'S
ITALIAN
MY FATHER'S
JEWISH
I'M IN
& THERAPY!

COOKBOOK

Compiled • Tested • Edited
Jane Evers

StarGroup
INTERNATIONAL INC

StarGroup International, Inc.
West Palm Beach, Florida
www.stargroupinternational.com

www.italianjewishtherapy.com

FIRST EDITION

Compiled • Tested • Edited by Jane Evers
Cover & Book design by Mel Abfier

Library of Congress Cataloging-in-Publication
My Mother's Italian, My Father's Jewish and I'm in Therapy Cookbook
ISBN 1-884886-82-5

Table of Contents

My Mother's Italian Recipes

Appetizers

Soups

Salads

Main Entrees

Pasta & Risotto

Vegetables

Desserts

My Father's Jewish Recipes

Appetizers

Soups

Salads

Entrees

Vegetables

Starches

Desserts

Hi, I'm Steve,

What better way to get to know my crazy family. You can always find us around a kitchen or dining room table. My Mom, grandma, Bubbie all my Aunts even some of my uncles had their signature dish.

Since writing the play, I've realize how much food has been a happy part of my live. I've asked my family and friends to contribute to this cookbook. Some recipes have been in my family for years others are fairly new. Most have been adjusted and tested by Jane for simplicity in cooking and, despite by objections, tailored towards healthy eating.

You will find no schmaltz, heavy oils, limited sugar and less salt than the normal Jewish or Italian recipes. Jane's adapted the recipes to help keep our cholesterol and sugar levels in balance.

I know many of my relatives would not approve of these changes, but new dietary guidelines and our healthier living styles make these changes necessary – At least, by following these recipes, your indigestion and gastric reflux will be under more control.

In any event, the recipes are authentic, developed with love of tradition and are really very delicious. So, my friends, enjoy, essen, manga...

Steve

Hi, I'm Jane.

I live with Steve. These last few years have really been a trip. How many people over 55 get the chance to live their dream? Here's how Steve & I arrived at Broadway's door:

In 1999, Steve & I were living in New York creating marketing projects for the cable & telecommunication industries. On weekends, Steve played the local comedy clubs. As projects were ending, I asked Steve if he wanted to pursue his dream of being a "working" comedian. "Working," in the comedy vernacular, means making a living.

Realizing that he couldn't compete with the young comedians in NYC, we needed to find a place where age would not be a detriment. Florida was chosen. We sold everything, packed our car, and with enough money to last a year, we moved. Thinking back, it was a pretty gutsy step, but I had total confidence in Steve's comedic talent.

For the first few years, I worked (I have an MBA and got a great job as a corporate communications director) and Steve played the condos. In 2001, he was picked up by a management group. Soon, management introduced him to The William Morris Agency. "My Mother's Italian, My Father's Jewish & I'm in Therapy" was born in 2003. After the show toured the country for two years, the idea of bringing it to Broadway was discussed. The Broadway management team was developed, paperwork completed, and investors secured.

About a year ago, I decided to contribute something to Steve's Broadway debut. I have no acting or comedic talents, anyone can tell you that, but I love to cook. What about a cookbook, I thought? And so, this cookbook was developed & written with lots of love, hopes & dreams. Now, it's completed and the show opens on November 3, 2006. What a journey! I know from experience that when you follow your heart, at any age, your dreams can come true.

Jane

Foreword

When my Grandma Angelina and my momma got into the kitchen to start cooking for a holiday it was like watching a SWAT team preparing for an assault. Dad and Uncle Paulie ("the mental midget" as momma called him) would return from the grocer, we didn't have super-markets per se back then, with the ammunition; fresh everything.

My cousin and I would stand close by the kitchen, like seagulls hovering over a picnic, waiting for scraps. I never remembered either my Momma or Grandma referring to a recipe. They had unusual words for measuring purposes. They used words like: pinch, schkootch, smidge, a lilla more. Measuring ingredients was more of an art rather than a science; taste and color and textures determined need. Too much salt? Throw in a potato. Too bitter? Pour in sugar (and I do mean pour) Too dark? Add water. And, amazingly enough, the final product was always the same as when they cooked it 25 years ago. Well... in truth, if it tasted different, no one had the balls to mention it to Grandma. It amazed me that Uncle Paulie, 325 pounds, 5'8 inches tall (Grandma was 4'7") could lift a car to change its tire, had to shave three times a day... would cry if Grandma yelled at him. "PAULIE!!!!" everybody got quiet. I remembered the time Uncle Paulie was almost vanquished from the family when he committed one of the worst acts of terrorism anyone could do against an Italian family... Grandma found a jar of Chef Boyardee in his fridge. He's still going to confession about it.

Her best food quote? I asked Grandma why Italians eat snails. She looked up from the spaghetti steam..."They don't like fast food!"

Acknowledgements

Thanks to everyone who was a part of this exciting adventure. Gladys Solomon, Steve's mother & Shelly Kaplan, Steve's sister gave me family recipes and told me hilarious stories about Steve's youthful eating habits. They haven't changed too much. Let me tell you, he's not the easiest person to cook for.

To Malvina Evers, my mother, & Ruth Evers, my sister, thanks for all the encouragement, the editing and tasting all those strange concoctions. What would I do without my great friend Marcia Davis, who's not the greatest cook, but the bestest friend, Susan Kobitz, & Lynette Lee, who came over to test recipes with me, but wouldn't take any leftovers home. I wonder why? Seth Goldberg, my son, who opened his catering kitchen to me for testing recipes and made terrific suggestions and Clara Goldberg, my granddaughter, who decided, as we were testing recipes, that she wanted to be a vegetarian. It truly wasn't my fault that the realization of where meat came from was discovered in the test kitchens.

And Steven, nothing would be anything without you. I am so proud of your zeal, persistence, and success. Building this life with you is exciting, challenging and always astonishing. Thanks for loving & sharing this journey with me.

Some basic items needed in an Italian Kitchen

Canned tomatoes
Diced, crushed, whole plum, sauce, paste.
Have a variety of can sizes

Cheese
Parmesan, mozzarella, ricotta, mascarpone

Seasonings
Oregano, basil, thyme, parsley (fresh or dried), capers, saffron, anchovies, bay leaf, rosemary

Nuts
Pine, almond

Wine
Marsala, Madicra, Brandy

Vinegar
Balsamic, white wine, red wine

Soups
Chicken, vegetable, beef broth

Vegetables
Spinach, zucchini, eggplant, carrots, onions, garlic, celery, olives, dried porcini mushrooms, chili peppers

Oils
Olive, vegetable

Pasta Variety (see page 46)

Ask a real Italian about their sauce and they know you're NO Italian. Real Italians call it gravy. If I called it sauce in front of Grandma Angelina, she'd say I was hanging out with a bad crowd. I also learned that oregano, the staple spice in every Italian house, adds aroma rather than taste. Grandma taught me lots of great kitchen tidbits. I did have one problem; I hated garlic. My Mom and Grandma found out one day while they watched me pick garlic pieces out of the sauce... sorry, gravy. Grandma went berserk. "Stoonahd! ...Doena you know Garlic isa good for you. Garlic, she makes a you bloodpressa - ho-kay... How my gonna teacha you... you so stubborn... Eata right and Dat means plenty garlic... ana you live long!. "But Grandma", I said... "You told me Grandpa Mario died when he was only 48". She made a face, growled, bit her finger, grabbed the wooden spoon and I suddenly remembered I had to clean out my sock drawer immediately.

I walked into Grandma's kitchen and watched her on a rickety chair with a mop in her hand, washing the ceiling. The ceiling? I later came to realize that Italians, all Italian, talk with their hands... even when they're holding a wooden spoon covered with spaghetti sauce.

MY MOTHER'S ITALIAN RECIPES

Think, for a moment about the sole purpose of an "appetizer." It's priming –the –pump The APPETIZER... getting things ready for the main event. These stuffed mushrooms are the main event. Just the smell of them baking in the oven is all the appetizer you'll need. Just one taste and save room for the main dish. Or, finish these delights and have the main dish tomorrow. Bon Appetito

Italian Appetizers

Start your engines

Baked Brie with Pest & Pine Nuts
Crab Salad Puffs
Italian Appetizer Loaf
Stuffed Mushrooms
Three-Cheese Spinach Calzones

Let's get serious here, my Grandma Angelina and my Momma never cooked with brie. Chances are, they never heard of brie. In fact, I never heard of brie until I was an adult. So, if Jane's going to try to convince the Italian side of my family that this is an Italian dish... Ok, she added pine nuts. That's a little Italian. Grandma tasted this, loved it and suddenly recalled an ancient family recipe called: Formaggio e Dadi di Pino con Pesto. (Baked brie with pine nuts and Pesto)

Nice try Grandma!

Baked Brie with Pesto and Pine Nuts or Baked Brie with Seedless Raspberry Jam and Pine Nuts

Oven baking at 450 degrees
Serves 8 - 10

Ingredients

1 (8 ounce) wheel Brie cheese
1 tablespoon Pesto Seasoning (1/2 teaspoon each of basil, parsley garlic)
1 tablespoon olive oil
1 tablespoon pine nuts
Ground Black Pepper
Frozen or refrigerated pie crust
Non-stick butter or olive oil spray
Assorted crackers

Need to buy:
• Brie
• Pine nuts
• Raspberry jam
• Frozen pie crust

Directions

1. Preheat oven to 450 degrees F.
2. Using a sharp knife, trim the white rind off top of the Brie (top part only, leaving the sides and bottom intact).
3. Defrost one pie crust & place Brie on it. Put into an 8 or 9-inch pie plate or ovenproof dish.
4. Use either the mixed pesto seasoning with olive oil, pine nuts, and garlic or the raspberry jam & chopped pine nuts.
5. Spread either mixture evenly over the top of the Brie round (where white rind was trimmed off). Sprinkle with black pepper (on pesto only) to taste, if desired.
6. Bring the edges of the pie crust up to meet and pinch together. Spray with non-stick spray.
7. Bake 12 minutes or until pie crust is browned.
8. Serve immediately; surround with assorted crackers.

Crab Salad Puffs

Oven baking if using frozen
pastries
Serves 4

Need to buy:
• Lump crabmeat
• Fresh parsley
• Coriander seeds
• Fresh/frozen
   puff pastries
• Mixed salad
   greens

Ingredients

1 can lump crabmeat
Juice of 1 - 2 lemons
1 tablespoon extra-virgin
   olive oil
2 teaspoons mayonnaise
2 teaspoons Dijon mustard
2 teaspoons honey
5 drops of Tabasco sauce (optional)
1 small bunch parsley, minced
Salt and freshly ground pepper
Coriander seeds, crushed
8 pre-made pastry puffs (I buy frozen pastries & bake
   them to order)
Pre-washed salad greens

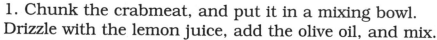

1. Chunk the crabmeat, and put it in a mixing bowl.
Drizzle with the lemon juice, add the olive oil, and mix.
2. Add the mayonnaise, mustard, honey, minced parsley
and season with salt, pepper and a pinch of coriander
seeds to taste. Mix in Tabasco (optional).
3. Cut the puffs in half, and scoop out a bit of the inside
to make room. If using frozen pastries, follow instruction
on box.
4. Fill each puff with a spoonful of the crab meat salad.
5. Arrange greens on a serving plate, and arrange the filled
puffs on top.
6. Drizzle any remaining sauce over pastries.

Italian Appetizer Loaf

Oven at 350 degrees
Serves 6 – 8

Ingredients:

1 pkg. frozen white bread
   dough
   (usually 3 loaves)
1 pound Mozzarella cheese,
   shredded
1/2 pound hard salami or pepperoni
Italian seasoning or oregano
1/4 cup butter, melted or
   butter spray
Poppy or sesame seed

Need to buy:
• Frozen white
  bread dough
• Mozzarella
• Hard Salami or
  pepperoni

1. Thaw 2 loaves of dough according to directions (can be done in microwave).
2. On floured surface, roll out 1 loaf of dough into approximately 10 x 15 inch rectangle. Brush or spray with butter.
3. Spread 1/2 of cheese and 1/2 of meat. Sprinkle with Italian seasoning. Roll up, starting at long end, seal the ends. Brush with butter and sprinkle with poppy or sesame seed.
4. Make about 12 cuts across roll, about 1 inch deep. Repeat this with second loaf.
5. Let rise about 1 hour in a warm place (warm, but turned off oven is good.)
6. Bake at 350 degrees for 25 to 30 minutes.

Stuffed Mushrooms

Oven at 350 degrees
Serves 4 – 6

Ingredients:

1/2 pound mild or hot
   Italian sausage
1/2 cup finely chopped onion
1/ green pepper, finely diced
1/8 teaspoon garlic powder
1/8 cup dry bread crumbs
1/8 teaspoon salt
dash of pepper
2/3 cup marinara or spaghetti sauce
20 large mushroom caps
3 tablespoons olive oil or use olive oil spray
shredded mozzarella cheese

Need to buy:
• Mild or hot sausage
• Mushrooms
• Mozzarella Cheese

1. Mix together the sausage, onion, green pepper, garlic powder.
2. Sauté in a skillet, then drain off the fat. Add in the bread crumbs, salt, pepper and spaghetti sauce.
3. Next, coat the mushroom caps with olive oil. Fill the mushroom caps with meat mixture.
4. Put the caps onto a cookie sheet, cover with foil and bake at 350F about 20 minutes.
5. Sprinkle the caps with mozzarella cheese and broil until cheese is melted and mushrooms are tender.

Three-Cheese Spinach Calzones

Oven at 425 degrees
Makes 2 calzones (serves 4)

Ingredients

1 10-ounce package frozen
   chopped spinach, thawed, &
   squeezed dry (do not cook)
3 green onions, chopped
1/2 cup part-skim ricotta cheese
1/4 cup crumbled Gorgonzola
1 cup (packed) grated or mozzarella
All purpose flour
*1 10-ounce tube refrigerated pizza dough
Non-stick spray

Need to buy:
• Frozen chopped spinach
• Green onions/ scallions
• Ricotta, Mozzarella, Gorgonzola cheese
• Pizza dough

1. Preheat oven to 425°F.
2. Mix spinach, onions, ricotta, Gorgonzola in medium bowl to blend. Season with salt and pepper.
3. Sprinkle heavy large baking sheet with flour. Unfold dough on prepared sheet.
4. **Gently stretch and/or roll dough to 11-inch square; cut in half diagonally, forming 2 triangles.
5. Place half of filling in center of each triangle.
6. Fold 1 side of each triangle over filling, forming 2 triangular calzones.
7. Press edges of dough to seal. Cut 3 slits in top of each to allow steam to escape. Spray with non-stick butter or olive oil flavor spray.
8. Bake calzones until golden brown, about 15 minutes; serve hot.

Italian Soups
It ain't just minestone anymore

Chilled Tomato Soup with Zucchini & Ricotta
Italian Bean & Sausage Soup
Lentil Soup with Escarole & Pancetta
Stracciatella
Zuppe Toscana

Chilled Tomato Soup with Zucchini and Ricotta

Stove top cooking
Serves 4

Ingredients

1 zucchini
2 tablespoons olive oil
1- 32 ounce can whole
  plum tomatoes
6 slices white sandwich bread,
  crusts removed, cubed
salt and freshly ground pepper
1/4 cup heavy cream
8 ounces fresh ricotta
julienne carrot
yellow bell peppers for garnish

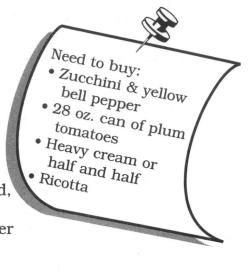

Need to buy:
• Zucchini & yellow bell pepper
• 28 oz. can of plum tomatoes
• Heavy cream or half and half
• Ricotta

1. Peel the zucchini. Julienne the peel, and reserve for garnish. Julienne carrot & yellow pepper for garnish too.
2. In a skillet over medium heat, warm 1 tablespoon of olive oil & add diced zucchini, saute 5 min.
3. Pour tomatoes and bread into a food processor. While processing, add the heavy cream in a slow, steady stream.
4. Distribute the sautéed zucchini among individual bowls, and pour the tomato-bread - cream soup on top.
5. Place ricotta in a bowl, and stir in 1 tablespoon of olive oil.
6. Put a dollup of ricotta on surface of soup.
7. Garnish with zucchini, carrots & yellow pepper.

Italian Bean and Sausage Soup

Stove top cooking
Serves 6

Need to buy:
• Italian sweet sausage
• Can plum tomatoes
• Pasta shells
• Can cannelloni beans

Ingredients

12 ounce sweet Italian sausage
2 teaspoon olive oil
1 cup chopped onion
2 teaspoon minced garlic
1 can (28 oz.) whole plum tomatoes
3 1/2 cup hot water
2 cups cooked medium pasta shells (4 oz.)
2 chicken bouillon cubes (or 2 teaspoons broth granules)
1 (19 ounce) can Cannelloni (white kidney beans) or other
   white beans

1. Remove sausage from casing. Crumble sausage into oil,
stir in onions and garlic. Cook over high heat, stirring
often until sausage browns.
2. Cut up tomatoes. Add tomatoes and the juice, water,
pasta and bouillon cubes to pot.
3. Bring to a boil over high heat. Reduce heat. Cover and
simmer 7 minutes.
4. Rinse and drain beans. Add to soup and simmer until
pasta is tender.

Talk about a hearty soup. Remember when they said if you eat that... "it'll put hair on your chest..." Well, my Uncle Paulie must have grown up on this soup. He's got a rug on his chest. One caveat... Lots of people, eating lots of this soup in a small room... need I go into details again? As Momma always said to me, "mangiate come una mucca." (you eat like a cow) I don't know what that has to do with Italian Bean and Sausage Soup. It just came to mind. Enjoy

Lentil Soup with Escarole and Pancetta

Stove top cooking
Serves 4 to 6

Ingredients

2 tablespoons olive oil
4 slices of pancetta, finely chopped
1 small onion, finely chopped
2 cloves of garlic, minced
2 carrots, finely diced
2 stalks of celery, finely chopped
2 cups green lentils
1 cup, chopped canned tomatoes
1 bay leaf
1 1/2 quarts chicken or vegetable broth
salt & pepper
1 teaspoon dried Italian seasonings
2 slices white bread Cut Into 1 inch cubes, no crusts
1/2 head escarole, washed, dried, and chopped
1 tablespoon balsamic vinegar
parmesan cheese

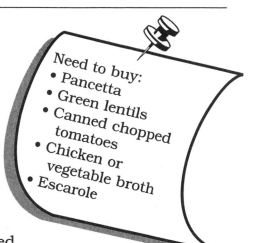

Need to buy:
• Pancetta
• Green lentils
• Canned chopped tomatoes
• Chicken or vegetable broth
• Escarole

1. Heat the olive oil with the pancetta, and cook until it is no longer pink.
2. Add the onions, celery, carrots, and garlic over medium heat until they are tender.
3. Add the lentils, tomatoes, chicken broth, salt, pepper and bay leaf. Bring to a boil and then reduce the heat to a simmer. Cook over low heat, adding water as needed until the lentils are tender, about 40 minutes.
4. Add the bread to the soup, and to thicken the soup.
5. Add the escarole and cook 5 minutes.
6. Stir in the balsamic vinegar.
7. Serve topped with a drizzle of olive oil and some grated parmesan cheese.

Stracciatella

Stove top cooking
Serves 4

Ingredients

3 cups chicken broth
3 eggs
1/4 cup fresh bread crumbs
1/4 cup parmesan cheese
salt & pepper
4 tablespoons fresh, chopped parsley

Need to buy:
• Parmesan cheese
• Fresh parsley

1. In a saucepan, bring the broth to a boil.
2. In a bowl, beat together the eggs, bread crumbs and cheese. Add salt and pepper.
3. Remove the broth from the heat, and pour in the egg mixture, stirring constantly.
4. Pour the soup into four separate bowls, and sprinkle with the parsley, and additional cheese if desired.

Note: Pastina (small pasta) may also be added to this soup.

Zuppa Toscana

Stove top cooking
Serves 4 to 6

Ingredients

4 links turkey sausage
  (spicy or mild)
1 medium onion,
  finely diced
3 strips of bacon, chopped
2 garlic cloves, peeled
  and minced
2 medium potatoes. peeled and cut
  into large dice
2 to 3 cups of chopped greens (kale or spinach)
salt & pepper to taste
1/4 cup heavy cream or half & half
4 cups chicken broth
parmesan cheese to serve

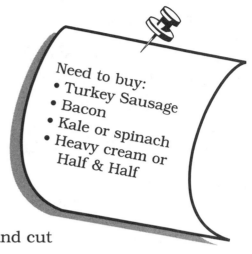

Need to buy:
• Turkey Sausage
• Bacon
• Kale or spinach
• Heavy cream or Half & Half

1. Cook the bacon in a heavy pan until crisp. Remove to another dish, leaving the bacon fat in the pan.
2. Add the sausage links, and cook over medium heat until browned well on all sides. Add 1/2 cup of water, cover, and cook another 10 minutes over medium low heat or until completely cooked.
3. Remove the sausages to a plate, and cook the onions in the same pan until translucent. Add the garlic, and cook another minute or two.
4. In a large soup or stockpot, add the chicken broth and potatoes. Bring to a boil, and then reduce the heat to medium low.

5. Cut the sausage links into 1/2 inch slices, and then add these to the stockpot. Cook for 10 minutes and then add the kale and bacon. Season with salt and pepper, and simmer another 10 minutes.

6. Remove a little of the potato from the pot, and place it in a bowl. Mash the potato together with the cream, and then add this mixture to the pot, mixing well.

7. Serve hot, offering a sprinkle of grated Parmesan cheese if desired.

Breads

Fresh toasted garlic bread, smothered in fresh butter, crunchy, just out of the oven. It was a meal in itself. When Momma brought out that basket of joy and placed it on the table, everyone dove for the first piece. There was never enough because you couldn't stop. On a good day, Momma made four gigantic toasted Italian garlic breads. By the end of the meal there wasn't a morsel left.

It doesn't get "breadder" than this.

I don't know why Jane didn't include this recipe in the book because Italian wedding soup is sooooo good. It's a blend of Chinese egg-drop soup, Italian mini meatballs and spinach. Wait, don't get excited, you won't even notice the spinach. It adds color and just the right touch of flavor. You might say, momma's Italian wedding soup is:.... a marriage of cultures and tastes. That joke was bad but the soup's fantastic. Don't tell Jane that I raided Mom's cookbook and have added this recipe.

Mini Meatballs:
1/2 pound meat loaf mix (ground beef and pork)
2 teaspoons dried parsley
1/4 cup grated Parmesan cheese (don't tell Steve)
1/4 teaspoon salt
1/8 teaspoon pepper
1 clove garlic, crushed
1/4 teaspoon oregano
1/4 teaspoon basil
1/4 cup milk

Combine the ingredients above. Form small 1/2 inch balls. Drop into boiling salted water. Simmer for 10 minutes, remove with a straining spoon, place on paper towels to drain briefly, refrigerate. Pour 3 quarts of chicken in soup pot. Add 1 head escarole, torn into bite sized pieces, black pepper, and red pepper flakes, to taste. Simmer 20 minutes. Meanwhile, break spaghetti into 4 inch long pieces and cook according to package directions. Drain. Add 1 1/2 cups cooked chicken and the meatballs to broth. Simmer 10 minutes more. You can substitute white cannelloni beans, ham or proscuitto for the chicken.

Mange

Italian Salads

The "Roto-Rooter" of course

Grilled Vegetable Pasta Salad
Marinated Vegetable Salad
Panzanella (Bread Salad)
Roma Tomato Salad
Vegetable Salad with Gorgonzola Dressing

Grilled Vegetable Pasta Salad

Stove top cooking
Grill or oven at 450 degrees
Serves 6

Ingredients

1 small zucchini or yellow summer squash, cut
   into 1-inch slices
8 cherry tomatoes
1 medium onion, cut into eighths
1 package (8 ounces) fresh mushrooms
2 tablespoons canola oil
2 tablespoons olive oil
2 teaspoons sugar or equivalent sweetener
1/2 teaspoon each, oregano, basil garlic power, onion
   powder, paprika
1/2 cup low fat salad dressing
salt & pepper to taste
8 ounces elbow macaroni
1/3 cup cold water

1. Toss zucchini, tomatoes, onion, mushrooms and next
five ingredients in a large bowl until well coated.
2. Brush grill rack lightly with vegetable oil, or spray with
cooking spray. Heat coals or gas grill for direct heat.
Place vegetables on grill, using slotted spoon. Grill uncovered 4 to 6 inches from medium heat 4 to 5 minutes,
turning once and brushing with remaining dressing in
bowl, until crisp-tender. Or you can bake at 450 degrees in
oven. Refrigerate vegetables uncovered in single layer while
making pasta.
3. Empty macaroni into large pan 2/3 full of boiling water.
Gently boil uncovered 12 minutes, stirring occasionally.
4. Using same bowl with any remaining dressing & salad
dressing, stir together; set aside.

5. Drain pasta; rinse with cool water. Shake to drain well.
6. Cut grilled vegetables in half if desired; stir vegetables and pasta into seasoning mixture.
7. Serve immediately, or refrigerate.

Need to buy:
- Zucchini, or yellow squash
- Cherry tomatoes
- Mushrooms, any kind
- Elbow macaroni

Marinated Vegetable Salad

No cooking
Serves 6 – 8

Ingredients

2 medium ripe tomatoes or
    4 Roma tomatoes cut in wedges
1 medium green pepper cut
    in small squares
1 small zucchini or yellow
    summer squash, thinly sliced
1/4cup tiny sliced red onion
2 tablespoons snipped fresh parsley
2 tablespoons olive oil
2 tablespoons balsamic vinegar or whine vinegar
2 tablespoons water
1 tablespoon snipped fresh thyme or basil, or 1 teaspoon
dried thyme or basil, crushed
1 clove garlic, minced
1 tablespoon pine nuts, toasted (optional)

Need to buy:
• Roma tomatoes, green pepper
• Zucchini or yellow squash
• Fresh parsley, thyme
• Pine nuts

1. In a large bowl combine tomatoes, green pepper,
zucchini or summer squash, onion, and parsley.
2. For dressing, in a screw-top jar combine oil, vinegar,
water, thyme or basil, and garlic. Cover and shake well.
Pour dressing over vegetable mixture. Toss lightly to coat.
3. Let mixture stand at room temperature for 30 to 60
minutes, stirring occasionally. If desired, stir in the pine
nuts. Serve with slotted spoon.

Make-Ahead Tip: Prepare salad. Cover and chill for at
least 4 hours or up to 24 hours, stirring once or twice.
Allow to stand at room temperature about 30 minutes
before serving. If desired, stir in pine nuts before serving.

Panzanella

(Bread Salad)

No cooking
Serves 4

Ingredients

2 cups day-old Italian bread torn into
    bite-size pieces or cut into 1-inch cubes
1 pound tomatoes, seeded and coarsely chopped
1/2 medium red onion, cut into thin wedges
    and separated
1/2 small cucumber, peeled and cut into chunks
1/4 cup snipped fresh basil
2 tablespoons snipped fresh parsley
2 cloves garlic, minced
2 tablespoons red or white wine vinegar
2 tablespoons olive oil
1/4 teaspoon salt
1/4 teaspoon pepper
Torn mixed greens (about 4 cups)

1. In a large mixing bowl combine bread cubes, chopped tomatoes, onion, cucumber, basil, parsley, and minced garlic.
2. For dressing, in a glass measure, stir together vinegar, olive oil, salt, and pepper; spoon over salad. Toss gently to coat.
3. Let stand for 15 minutes to allow the flavors to blend.
4. Serve over torn greens.

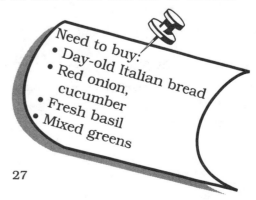

Need to buy:
• Day-old Italian bread
• Red onion,
  cucumber
• Fresh basil
• Mixed greens

Roma Tomato Salad

No cooking
Serves 4 – 6

Ingredients

3 pounds Roma tomatoes, in wedges
2 medium sweet onion, thinly sliced
3 cloves garlic, minced
1/4 cup of olive oil
1/4 cup red wine vinegar
1/4 cup fresh basil torn in small pieces
1 teaspoon mixed Italian herbs (oregano, basil, garlic
   powder, onion powder - 1/4 teaspoon each)
Salt and pepper (to taste)
2 scallions chopped (garnish)

1. Combine tomatoes and onions.
2. Prepare dressing by mixing the rest of the ingredients
together.
3. Toss together and store n refrigerator for one day. Don't
forget to mix the salad a few times.
4. Serve on a bed of lettuce or mixed greens with scallions
as garnish.

Need to buy:
• Roma tomatoes
• Sweet onions
• Fresh basil
• Scallions

Vegetable Salad with Gorgonzola Dressing

Stove top cooking
Serves 4

Ingredients

12 ounces string beans, trimmed
2 ripe medium tomatoes
4 ounces Gorgonzola cheese, crumbled
4 ounces plain yogurt
1 tablespoon extra-virgin olive oil
salt & freshly ground pepper
6 ounces canned corn, drained
Paprika for dusting

1. Bring a large pot of water to a boil. Add salt and the string beans, and cook until just tender, about 3 to 4 minutes.
2. Remove from the water, and plunge into an ice bath. Drain the string beans, and set aside.
3. Cut the tomatoes into wedges, and set aside.
4. Place the Gorgonzola in a large bowl, and add the yogurt and olive oil.
5. Season with salt and pepper, and mix well until it's a smooth, creamy dressing.
6. Pour over tomatoes and string beans. Toss gently. Serve immediately.

Need to buy:
• String beans
• Ripe tomatoes
• Yogurt
• Gorgonzola cheese

Having grown up in a home where eating took precedence over everything, I was rather dismayed when I found out that my new bride now my ex new bride, couldn't cook. That's not to say that she didn't try. Since Mama & Grandma had set culinary standards, they were a tough act to follow. My ex would try to replicate some of my family's secret recipes. The problem became apparent when, whatever she tried to make... even if she followed the recipe exactly, it always came out like Vito's blue plate special at the Main Street Diner. Something was amiss, "She shouldn't be that bad? I thought.

One day, in the middle of the same argument that I've been having with my Mom about my ex, she would present me with a litany of reasons why she was no good for me, held me back financially and most of all, couldn't cook. I asked my Mother how come, if she follows your recipe exactly, everything taste like crap? My mother shouted, "How should I know?" She must be doing something wrong. Then I noticed that my Mom bit her lip. That was the flashing neon sign that said Mom was lying. Being an adult I wasn't too afraid that she would hit me for being precocious so, since she was a foot & a half shorter than me, I cornered her and questioned her. She confessed. Grandma & Mama used to leave out parts of recipes so no one could duplicate their masterpieces exactly. A pinch of salt became... add some salt. A teaspoon became a tablespoon.
Blood IS thicker than water.

Italian Main Entrees
Hope you saved some room

Chicken Cacciatore
Italian Lemon Chicken
Chicken Marsala
Italian Meatloaf
Osso Buco

Mom used to make Chicken Cacciatore often. I really didn't like it; not because it didn't taste great... mom made it with whole chicken pieces... meat AND bones. And, since I was a "utensil-challenged" child; I ate the big pieces with my hands... And..., since Mom's Chicken Cacciatore was always smothered in Mom's special tomato sauce... Mr. Clean spray and Bounty was always handy. It was a bone chilling experience.

So, once again "necessity is the mother of invention" and, in that light, Jane came up with the same wonderful Chicken Cacciatore recipe BUT... the chicken has no bones. You might ask how can a chicken without bones walk? Seriously, it's terrific. No more fighting to get that last morsel of meat off the bones. No bones about it, this is a wonderful update on a delicious dish. That Jane doesn't have a bad bone in her body. Any of this hit your funny bone? OK, I'll stop.

Chicken Cacciatore with Fusilli

Stove top cooking
Serves 4

Ingredients

2 Tablespoons vegetable oil
2 Tablespoons olive oil
3 1/2-pounds boneless,
   chicken breast, or 3 pounds
   boneless, skinless chicken
   thighs or combination
1 onion, chopped fine
1/2 pound mushrooms, sliced thin
2 carrots, peeled and sliced
2 celery stacks, sliced
5 -6 garlic cloves, minced
28-ounce can diced tomatoes including the juice
1/2 cup dry red wine
2 flat anchovy fillets, rinsed, patted dry, and mashed
   to a paste
1 teaspoon dried mixed Italian seasonings, crumbled
1 pound Fusilli (corkscrew-shaped pasta)
1/2 cup minced fresh parsley leaves if desired

Need to buy:
• Chicken
• Mushrooms, any kind
• Dry red wine
• Anchovies
• Fusilli (corkscrew-shaped pasta)

1. In a kettle, heat the oil over moderately high heat
until it is hot but not smoking and brown the chicken, in
batches, transferring it as it is browned to a bowl.
2. Pour off and discard all but about 3 tablespoons of the
oil and in the remaining oil cook the onions and the mushrooms over moderate heat, stirring occasionally, until the
onions are golden.
3. Add the carrots, celery, garlic and cook the mixture,
stirring, for 1 minute. Add the tomatoes with the juice, the
wine, the chicken with any juices that have accumulated

in the bowl, the anchovy paste, and the Italian seasonings and simmer the mixture, covered, stirring occasionally and breaking up the tomatoes, for 30 to 35 minutes, or until the chicken is tender.

4. The chicken mixture may be made 2 days in advance. Reheat the chicken mixture before serving.

5. In kettle of boiling salted water cook the fusilli for 10 to 12 minutes, or until it is al dente, drain it well, and in a large bowl toss it with the chicken mixture.

6. Sprinkle the chicken cacciatore with the parsley.

Italian Lemon Chicken

Stove top cooking
Serves 4

Ingredients

4 skinless chicken breasts,
   pounded flat flour to coat
1 teaspoon olive oil
1/2 cup drinking sherry
   or dry white wine
juice of 2 lemon, no seeds!
zest of one lemon
1 Tablespoon sugar
1/2 cup chicken broth
2 tablespoons butter
1 1/4 teaspoons Italian herbs (basil, oregano)
1/4 - 1/2 cup Italian parsley, chopped
1 tablespoon minced garlic
Salt and Pepper, to taste

Need to buy:
• Chicken breast
• Lemons
• Dry wine or sherry
• Parsley

1. Pound chicken flat and coat the chicken in flour and shake off excess.
2. Heat the olive oil in sauté pan over medium high heat.
3. Sauté the chicken about two minutes on each side, just until it is browned on the outside.
4. Add the wine or sherry to deglaze the pan, and scrape the browned bits off the bottom of the pan and it will be an integral part of the lemon chicken.
5. Add garlic, lemon juice, pepper, Italian herbs, butter, and chicken broth, and sauté for approximately two minutes.
6. Add the chicken back in and sauté until the chicken is done, about fifteen minutes.
7. Sprinkle with chopped parsley and serve.

Chicken Marsala•

Stove top cooking
Serves 4

Ingredients

1/4 cup all-purpose flour
   for coating
1/2 teaspoon salt
1/4 teaspoon ground black pepper
*4 skinless, boneless chicken breast
4 - 6 tablespoons olive oil
1 1/2 cups sliced mushrooms
1/2 & 3/4 cups Marsala wine
1/4 cup balsamic vinegar
1/4 – 1/2 cup fresh parsley chopped

Need to buy:
• **Boneless chicken breasts
• Fresh parsley
• Sliced mushrooms
• Marsala wine
• Balsamic vinegar

1. In a shallow dish or bowl, mix together the flour, salt, pepper.
2. Lightly coat chicken pieces in flour mixture.
3. In a large skillet, heat oil over medium-high heat. Place chicken in the pan, and lightly brown on both sides.
4. Take out chicken pieces and place in bowl. Add mushrooms to the pan and cook until limp (3 – 5 minutes). Flash with 1/2 cup wine.
5. Put chicken back in pan. Add another 3/4 cup wine, balsamic vinegar and some salt & pepper. Lower heat.
6. Cover skillet; simmer chicken on low-medium heat for 15 minutes, turning once, until chicken is no longer pink and juices run clear.
7. Sprinkle with parsley.

*NOTE: You can use chicken, veal even thinly sliced beef for this dish. Each portion should be between 4 – 6 ounces.

Italian Meat Loaf or Meat Balls

Oven at 350 degrees
Serves 8

Meat Loaf Ingredients

2 1/2 pounds lean hamburger
or chopped turkey
2 cups canned diced tomatoes
2 eggs, beaten
1 cup onion, finely chopped
2 cups Italian bread crumbs
1/4 cup ketchup or chili sauce
1-2 tablespoons horseradish
1 tablespoon Dijon mustard

Need to buy:
* Hamburger meat
or chopped turkey
• Canned tomatoes
• Italian bread
crumbs
• Ketchup or chili
sauce
• Horseradish
• Dijon mustard

Spice Mix: 1 teaspoon of each: Oregano, dry mustard, thyme, garlic powder, onion powder, basil and freshly ground black pepper. Add 1 tablespoon kosher Salt. Mix it all together.
Dash or two of Tabasco (optional)
3 tablespoons Worcestershire sauce

Topping Ingredients

1/4 cup reduced homemade tomato sauce*
1/4 cup bottled grocery store chili sauce or ketchup
1/3 cup cheddar cheese, (or any of your favorite Italian cheeses).

Mix the ketchup or chili sauce and tomato sauce. You'll sprinkle the cheese over the sauce.

*NOTE: Put the tomato sauce in a sauce pan, add about 1 Tablespoon of lemon juice, 2 Tablespoon Worcestershire sauce, and about 1/4 cup of brandy. Reduce this into a near paste, and you'll really intensify the flavor of the tomato sauce.

Preparation Of The Meat Loaf

1. Preheat oven to 350 degrees.
2. Mix all of the ingredients, except the topping, in a large mixing bowl.
3. Then, place the mixture into a large bread pan and spread it evenly into a loaf.
4. Bake for about 1 hour. Drain off the excess liquid and "ice" it with the topping.
5. Bake about 15 more minutes, or until the cheese is toasted, and you'll be in for a gourmet treat.

Preparation of the Meat Balls:

Follow steps 1 & 2. Instead of putting in loaf pan, shape mixture into medium large balls. (Should make 16 – 20 balls). Place on cookie sheet and bake in oven about 25 - 30 minutes. Really crunchy outside.

Italian Osso Buco

Stove top
Serves 6 - 8

Ingredients

3 pounds veal shanks
  (see Note)
1/3 cup Marsala wine
  (or dry sherry)
3-4 teaspoons extra virgin
  olive oil
1/3 cup brandy
2 teaspoons butter or
  Butter Buds
1 tablespoon balsamic vinegar
1 red onion, coarsely chopped
2 tablespoons tomato paste
1/2 green bell pepper, coarsely chopped
1 sprig rosemary
1/2 red bell pepper, coarsely chopped
4 sprigs thyme
3 carrots, peeled and coarsely chopped
2 bay leaves
1 large stalk celery, coarsely chopped
2 cups chicken broth (canned or
5-6 cloves garlic, thinly sliced homemade)
Salt and pepper to taste

Need to buy:
• Veal shanks
• Green & red pepper
• Marsala wine & brandy
• Tomato paste
• Fresh rosemary, thyme
• Chicken broth

Gremolata (place on top of each serving):
2 tablespoon chopped Italian Parsley
1 clove garlic, minced
1/2 teaspoon grated lemon peel
1 teaspoon lemon juice
Mix in a bowl and reserve to sprinkle over individual
servings.

1. In a large skillet or Dutch oven with a tight-fitting lid, add 2 Teaspoons olive oil over medium high heat. Season shanks with salt and pepper on both sides, then brown them on all sides. When browning is down, remove the shanks to a bowl to be added back in later.

2. In the same pan, reduce heat to low and add 2 tablespoons olive oil and butter or Butter Buds. Add the onions, peppers, carrots, celery and garlic. Stir well to coat, then cover.

3. Simmer, stirring occasionally, for about 10 minutes. (This will allow the vegetables to release their juices)

4. Add the Marsala or sherry and the brandy, also the balsamic vinegar. Stir in well, cover again, and let simmer on low for about 6-8 minutes.

5. Make a "bouquet garni" out of the rosemary, thyme and bay leaves. (Wrap them in cheese cloth and tie with cooking twine.) Add this to the simmering vegetables, along with the tomato paste. Increase heat to medium-high and add the shanks and chicken, veal or beef stock. Stir both in well to mix with vegetables.

6. When broth is boiling, reduce heat to low again and cover. Cook for about 1-1 1/2 hours. Veal should be "falling off the bone" tender after an hour or less. Lamb or beef might take a full hour and a half to reach maximum tenderness. Falling off the bone is probably not going to happen with lamb or beef, but the meat should be very tasty and quite tender.

7. Garnish with gremolata.

Pasta

*The staple of an Italian family. Al Dente...
never undercooked. Italian logic. Eat five
servings of vegetables a day; you loose weight
and stay healthy. Pasta's made from wheat---
wheat's a vegetable---you do the math!*

Big and tall shop here we come.

Italian Pasta & Risotto
"Spagetti" never looked so good

Baked Pasta
Milanese Risotto
Pasta Variations on a Theme
Sausage & Wild Mushroom Risotto
Simply Lasagna

When I was growing up, we had spaghetti with...? It was spaghetti, just spaghetti. There was no Rigatoni, Fusilli, Penne, Ziti, Orzo,... Just plain old spaghetti. When did spaghetti become pasta? I think about the same time that Italian Restaurants became risterantes. D'Italiano. Then a bowl of spaghetti became a bowl of pasta and the price went up accordingly.

Baked Pasta

Stove top cooking
Oven at 350 degrees

Ingredients

1 pound cooked spaghetti or penne
32 ounces of spaghetti sauce (homemade or canned...
   don't tell Grandma)
Left over hamburger/chicken/sausage (optional)
Left over cooked vegetables
1 1/2 cups Ricotta
1 1/2 cups cubed mozzarella
8 ounces sliced mozzarella
1/2 cup grated cheese

1. Cook spaghetti or use left over.
2. Combine left over meat & vegetables with Ricotta, cubed mozzarella and sauce.
3. Pour over spaghetti and mix thoroughly.
4. Pour into greased baking pan.
5. Cover with sliced mozzarella cheese and bake at 350 degrees until bubbly.
6. Serve with grated cheese.

Need to buy:
• Ricotta
• Mozzarella

Pasta Variations on a Theme

Here's an idea that Jane uses all the time. She mixes &
matches different pasta, with a sauce, and throws in either
roasted veggies, meat, fish or poultry. The varieties are
endless. Just look at some of the pasta choices available.

Tubular Pasta: Bocconcini, Bucatini, Calamarata (cala-
mari), Calamarata (calamari), Canneroni, Cannelloni,
Cannolicchi,, Cellentani, Chifferi, Chifferini, Elbow maca-
roni, Elicoidali, Fagioloni, Garganelli, Gomiti, Macaroni,
Maccheroni, Maccheroncelli, Magliette, Maltagliati,
Manicotti, Mezzani Rigati, Mezze Penne, Mezzi
Bombardoni, Mezzi Paccheri, Mezzi Rigatoni, Mostaccioli,
Paccheri, Pasta al ceppo, Penne rigate, Penne Zita,
Pennette, Pennine rigate, Pennoni, Perciatelli, Reginelle,
Rigatoncini, Rigatoni, Sagne Incannulate, Spaccatelle,
Trenne, Trennette, Tortiglioni, Tufoli, Ziti – Cut, Ziti –
Long, Ziti rigati, Zitoni,

Strand Pasta: Angel Hair (capelli d' angelo), Barbina,
Bigoli, Capelli d'angelo (Angel Hair), Capellini, Chitarra
(spaghetti alla chitarra), Ciriole, Fedelini (fidelini), Fusilli
lunghi, Spaghetti, Spaghettini, Spaghettoni, Thin
Spaghetti, Vermicelli,

Ribbon Pasta Noodles: Bavette, Bavettine (mezze lin-
guine), Fettuce, Fettuccine, Fettucelle, Kluski, Lasagne,
Lasagnette, Lasagnotte, Linguettine, Linguine, Mafalde,
Mafaldine, Pappardelle, Pillus, Pizzoccheri, Reginette,
Riccia, Sagnarelli, Stringozzi, Tagliatelle, Taglierini (taglioli-
ni, tonnarelli), Trenette (trinette), Tripoline

Stuffed Pasta: Agnolotti, Cappelletti (alpine hats),
Cappelloni, Manti, Mezzaluna, Pansotti, Ravioli, Ravioloni,
Ravioletti, Tortelli (anolini), Tortellini, Tortelloni

Seth's Marinara Sauce (Gravy)

Ingredients

1 large white or yellow onion (diced)
2 tablespoons chopped garlic
3 tablespoons extra virgin olive oil
2 teaspoons salt (or to taste)
2 teaspoons pepper (or to taste)
1 tablespoon dried oregano
1 tablespoon dried basil
1 tablespoon dried parsley
1/2 teaspoon crushed red pepper (or to taste)
2 large cans (28 ounces) of tomato sauce

1. Dice and chop up the onion and garlic.
2. Put pot on stove and add the extra virgin olive oil to the bottom of the pan, heat at medium high for a minute before adding onions and garlic. Cook onions and garlic till translucent and/or slightly golden brown.
3. Next add all your dried ingredients (salt, pepper, oregano, basil, parsley and crushed red pepper) and mix with spoon, lower heat a little bit. Cook until the oil, onions, garlic and dried ingredients look like a paste or for about 5-7 minutes.
4. Next add your tomato sauce.
5. Lower heat to medium to medium low and let cook, while stirring occasionally.
6. Cook for a minimum of 1 hour and up to 6 hours in length.
7. Cool and use for any recipe that needs sauce/gravy.

Milanese Risotto

Stove top cooking
Serves 4 – 6

Ingredients

3 tablespoons olive oil
2 + 2 tablespoons butter
1 large onion, diced
1/4 cup white wine
1/2 teaspoon saffron threads, (optional)
1 cup Arborio rice
5-8 cups chicken stock
1/2cup pecorino romano cheese, shredded
1/4 cup Italian parsley, chopped, as garnish

Need to buy:
• Arborio rice sometimes called Italian rice
• Fresh parsley
• Saffron threads

1. Heat chicken stock to slowly simmering in a sauce pan.
2. Heat a large, heavy skillet over medium heat. Add olive oil and 2 tablespoons of butter.
3. When butter is just melted, add onions, stir to coat and sauté for 5 minutes. Add Arborio rice, stir to coat well, sprinkle in saffron threads.
4. Add wine and let absorb into rice.
5. Reduce heat to low and add enough stock to just cover the rice. Keep adding warm stock as needed to maintain covering. Continue this process for about 20 minutes, until rice is tender.
6. Allow last stock added to reduce until about 90 percent absorbed, then, add remaining 2 tablespoons butter. Stir in well.
7. Add pecorino romano and stir it in well.
8. Remove from heat and let rest for 5 minutes while final liquid is absorbed. Your risotto Milanese should be rich and creamy. Rice should be tender.

Sausage and Wild Mushroom Risotto

Stove top cooking
Serves 4 main or 8 side

Ingredients

2 tablespoons olive oil
1 pound Italian sweet sausage,
  casings removed, crumbled
  into 1/2-inch pieces
8 ounces portobello mushrooms,
  stemmed, dark gills
  scraped out, caps diced
10 ounces fresh shiitake mushrooms,
  stemmed, diced
1 teaspoon chopped fresh thyme
1 teaspoon chopped fresh oregano
1 1/2 cups Madeira
6 cups chicken stock or canned low-salt chicken broth
1/2 cup (1 stick) butter
1 large onion, chopped
4 garlic cloves, minced
2 cups arborio rice or other medium-grain rice
  (about 13 ounces)
1 cup freshly grated Asiago/parmesan cheese

Need to buy:
• Italian sweet sausage
• Mushrooms – Portobello/shitake
• Madeira wine
• Chicken stock
• Aborio rice
• Asiago or parmesan cheese

1. Heat oil in large nonstick skillet over medium-high heat. Add sausage and sauté until beginning to brown, about 3 minutes.
2. Add all mushrooms, thyme, and oregano and sauté until mushrooms are tender, about 10 minutes.
3. Add 1/2 cup Madeira; boil until almost absorbed, about 1 minute. Set aside.
4. Bring stock to simmer in large saucepan; remove from heat and cover to keep hot.

5. Melt butter in heavy large pot over medium-high heat. Add onion and garlic and sauté until onion is translucent, about 5 minutes.

6. Add rice; stir 2 minutes. Add remaining 1 cup Madeira; simmer until absorbed, about 2 minutes.

7. Add 1 cup hot stock; simmer until almost absorbed, stirring often, about 3 minutes. Continue to cook until rice is just tender and mixture is creamy, adding more stock by cupfuls, stirring often and allowing most stock to be absorbed before adding more, about 25 minutes.

8. Stir in sausage mixture. Season to taste with salt and pepper.

9. Transfer to serving bowl. Pass cheese separately.

You know that old adage: There's always room for Jello?" There's always room for Grandma's Lasagna... there better be. It was a miracle, a medley of flavors. I liked the meat lasagna the best. One never knew just what meat it was and one never asked. "Meat's meat!" She would say. I'm convinced it was usually yesterday's meat smothered in things that covered up any semblance of recognition. Veal? Pork? Kidneys? Who cared? It was always good, really good but you had to make room cause you never said no to Grandma's lasagna. And thanks to Grandma's food mandates; we had nine bulimics in the family. Coincidence? I think not!

Simply Lasagna

Stove top cooking & Oven at 375 degrees
Serves 8

Ingredients

1 pound lean ground beef
1/2 6 oz can (3 oz) tomato paste
1/2 medium sweet white onion,
   diced.
1 pound ricotta cheese
1/2 large green bell pepper,
   diced.
1 1/2 pounds mozzarella
   (large flat square slices)
1/2 pound dry lasagna noodles
3/4 pound freshly grated
   parmesan cheese
(9 lasagna noodles - unbroken)
2 teaspoons each, garlic power, oregano, Italian spice,
   parsley
1/4 cup sugar
1 teaspoon garlic, pinch of garlic salt
1 28 ounce can tomato sauce
1 garlic cloves, minced
16 ounces stewed tomatoes
white wine vinegar

Need to buy:
• Ground beef, turkey, chicken, veal, pork or combination.
• Ricotta & Mozzarella cheese
• Lasagna noodles
• Green pepper, onion
• Can of tomato sauce, tomato paste, sewed tomatoes
• Fresh parsley

1. Brown lean ground beef in skillet until lightly browned and cooked through. Remove and drain. Dispose of excess fat & wipe pan.
2. In same pan, add diced green pepper and onion to skillet. Brown for a few minutes on medium high heat, add browned beef back to the skillet, lower the heat to low and continue to cook for 5 more minutes stirring frequently.

3. Transfer browned beef, green pepper and onions to 3 quart. pot. Add tomato sauce & tomato paste. Open stewed tomatoes and dice, then add oregano, parsley, Italian Spice Mix to taste, probably 2 teaspoons of each. Add garlic and a pinch of garlic salt, to taste. Add a dash of white wine vinegar. Add sugar a couple tablespoons at a time, until desired level of sweetness, no more than 1/4 cup of sugar.
4. Stir and allow sauce to simmer 15-45 minutes to thicken (do not scorch bottom, stir frequently). Remove from heat.
5. Cook 1 pound lasagna noodles in 6 quart. Pot per cooking directions (al dente). (Note noodles may be cooked in advance.) Stir often to prevent from sticking, use low boil. Add 1 tablespoon oil & 1/2 teaspoon salt (if desired) to water. Drain in colander and place in cool water filled pan to keep from drying out and sticking together.
6. In dry lasagna pan, ladle one cup of sauce and spread along the bottom of the pan. Apply a layer noodles 3 length wise (edges overlapping). Ladle in sauce sparingly into center trough of 3 noodles. Apply a layer of mozzarella cheese slices on top of lasagna sauce. Place ricotta cheese dollops (about a tablespoon) every 2 inches in center of noodles on top of mozzarella cheese slices, sprinkle grated parmesan cheese in thin even layer on top of ricotta cheese.
7. Apply second layer of noodles going in the opposite direction. Repeat three times topping with noodles. If you have extra sauce and cheese you can spread that over the top. Tent lasagna pan with aluminum foil (not touching noodles or sauce). Allow to cool before serving.

Mom had strange ways of getting what she wanted. Sometimes I had to translate from momma to English. A poor translation on my part usually resulted in pain and suffering for me... case in point.

I'm sitting on the porch, reading a comic book; mom's sitting next to me and knitting names into a sweater... think "Dickens." Mom looks up, "You feel like an apple?" "No thanks mom." I answered. She continued, "I just-a bought fresh sweet apples, the kind-a you like." I looked up from the comic, "No, I'm good, I don't want one." Mom's nostrils started to flare, "Ow come, every time I buy you exactly want you want, you don't eat it. So you know what? Let them rot in the fridge. I'll just throw them out, waste Daddy's money, because you decide that you don't want exactly what I buy for you... I can't believe it... why do I bother?

I stood up. "Ok, Ok, I'll get an apple, I'll get an apple. Just as I started to walk into the kitchen mom shouts...

"While you up, bring me a..."

Italian Vegetables

These "sides" should be in the front

Baked Spinach
Eggplant Parmesan
Italian Zucchini Sauté
Pan/Oven-Fried Asparagus
Zucchini Pie

Baked Spinach

Stove top cooking
Oven at 350 degrees
Serves 4

Ingredients

1 1/2 teaspoon melted butter
1/2 cup chopped onions
1/4 cup parmesan cheese
3/4 cup ricotta cheese
1/4 teaspoon ground nutmeg
Salt and pepper to taste
1/8 teaspoon garlic powder
2 (10 ounces) pkgs. chopped spinach
1 (8 oz.) can tomato sauce
1/2 teaspoon oregano
1/2 teaspoon basil
1/2 cup shredded mozzarella cheese
    (optional)

Need to buy:
• Frozen chopped spinach
• Tomato or marinara sauce
• Ricotta & mozzarella cheese
• Nutmeg

1. Cook spinach only until separated. Drain well.
2. Melt butter in large skillet over medium-high heat. Add onions and sauté until golden. Remove from heat.
3. Stir in parmesan, ricotta, nutmeg, salt, pepper, garlic powder, onions and spinach.
4. Spoon into 9-inch pie pan that has been sprayed with a nonstick cooking spray. Smooth top of mixture with back of a spoon.
5. *Combine tomato sauce, oregano, and basil. Spread evenly over spinach mixture. Sprinkle mozzarella cheese over top.
6. Bake, uncovered, for 25 minutes in 350 degree oven.
7. Let stand 5 minutes before serving.

*NOTE: you can use a canned or homemade marinara sauce instead.

Eggplant Parmesan

Stove top cooking
Oven at 350 degrees
Serves 4

Need to buy:
- 32 ounce can crushed tomatoes
- Eggplant
- Parmesan & mozzarella cheese

Ingredients

2 tablespoons olive oil
1/4 cup mixture of
    vegetable oil/olive oil
1 garlic clove, minced
1 large onion, finely chopped
32 ounces bottled/canned
    crushed tomatoes
2 teaspoons sugar or sugar substitute
1/2 teaspoon oregano leaves
1/2 teaspoon salt
1 cup dried bread crumbs
2 eggs
1 large eggplant, peeled and cut into 1/2 inch slices (see note)
1/2 cup grated parmesan cheese
1 8-ounce mozzarella or monterey jack cheese cut grated or cut into 1/4 inch slices
2 tablespoon water

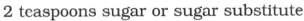

1. In 9-inch skillet over medium heat add 2 tablespoons oil, cook garlic and onion until tender, then add next 5 ingredients. Reduce heat; cook, covered, 30 minutes.
2. On waxed paper, place bread crumbs in small dish. With fork, beat eggs and water. Dip eggplant slices (after salting – see note) in egg then in bread crumbs. Repeat to coat slices twice.
3. Grease 13x9 inch baking dish. In 12 inch skillet over medium heat 1/4 cup mixed vegetable & olive oil, and

cook a few eggplant slices at a time till golden brown. Add oil as needed.

4. Preheat oven to 350 degrees. Arrange 1/2 eggplant slices in baking dish. Cover with 1/2 tomato mixture. Sprinkle with 1/2 parmesan and mozzarella cheese. Repeat. Bake 25 minutes.

Note: To make eggplant less bitter, after cutting sprinkle with salt and place on a wire rack one slice upon the other. Put something heavy on the top and let the bitter juices bleed out. After 30 minutes, wash the eggplant and proceed.

Italian Zucchini Sauté

Stove top cooking
Serves 4

Ingredients

1/4 cup olive oil
1 small white onion,
   sliced into thin wedges
1 (14.5 ounce) can diced tomatoes with juice
2 zucchini, sliced thin
i teaspoon each (oregano, basil & thyme)
1 teaspoon salt
1 teaspoon sugar

Need to buy:
• Can of diced tomatoes
• Zucchini

1. Heat the olive oil in a skillet over medium heat. Stir in onion and cook until tender.
2. Mix in tomatoes with juice and zucchini. Season with Italian seasoning and salt.
3. Cook and stir until zucchini is tender. Mix in sugar and adjust seasonings to taste.

Some things are not supposed to be limp when you want them hard... hey, where's your mind going here... I'm talking about vegetables. We never had fresh vegetables in the fridge. Fresh veggies have that "snap" that defines freshness; that crunch that echoes in your head as your chew. My ex specialized in limp veggies. There was nothing more inviting than munching on a floppy carrot. I used to complain but she saw nothing wrong with soft celery or mushy peppers. Everything she was involved with stayed limp...

I guess that's why she's my ex?

Pan or Oven-Fried Asparagus

Stove top or Oven at 450 degrees
Serves 4

Ingredients

1/4 cup butter or butter spray
2 tablespoons olive oil
1 teaspoon coarse salt
1/4 teaspoon ground black pepper
3 cloves garlic, minced
2 pounds fresh asparagus spears, trimmed

Need to buy:
• 2 pounds
• Asparagus

Version 1
1. Melt butter in a skillet over medium-high heat. Stir in the olive oil, salt, and pepper.
2. Cook garlic in butter for a minute, but do not brown.
3. Add asparagus, and cook for 10 minutes, turning asparagus to ensure even cooking.

Version 2 (no butter or oil)
1. Spray cookie sheet with butter or olive oil spray.
2. Lay asparagus in singe layer on cookie sheet & spray with oil.
3. Sprinkle coarse salt over and bake at 450 degrees for about 8 – 10 minutes.

Zucchini Pie

Oven at 350 degrees
Serves 6

Ingredients

3 cups very thinly sliced zucchini (4 medium zucchinis)
1/2 yellow onion, chopped
Handful parsley, chopped
3 cloves garlic, finely chopped
1 cup Bisquick or biscuit mix
1/2 cup vegetable oil
1/2 teaspoon marjoram
1/2 teaspoon seasoned salt
1/2 cup parmesan cheese
4 eggs, lightly beaten
Salt and pepper to taste

Need to buy:
• Zucchini
• Bisquick or equivalent

1. Mix dry ingredients in bowl.
2. Mix eggs, oil, zucchini and onions in large bowl.
3. Add dry ingredients to egg mixture.
4. Pour into a greased 9x13 pan. Preheat oven to 350 degrees & bake for 25 minutes.
5. Cool and cut into squares.

*Italian pastries - My family would
wait for dessert like feeding time at
the zoo. A fine cannoli, that Italian delicacy
with a crispy crust and a sweet cheesy
filling... well, my cousin Paulie would dunk it
into espresso and consider that a nutritious
breakfast. That was back then when he only
weighed 375 pounds.*

Italian Desserts

Did you eat all your veggies?

Biscuit Tortoni
Cantucci
Italian Cassata
Panna Cotta
Tiramisu

Bisque Tortoni

No cooking
Serves 4

Ingredients

2 cups vanilla ice cream.
   (The higher the fat content,
   the better)
1/4 cup mascarpone cheese
2 tablespoons almond paste
1/2 cup crumbled & sieved
   macaroons or almond cookies
1/2 cup mini-chocolate chips (optional)

Need to buy:
• Vanilla ice cream
• Mascarpone cheese
• Almond paste
• Macaroons or almond cookies
• Mini-chocolate chips

1. Slightly melt the vanilla ice cream. Start to beat.
2. Add the Mascarpone & almond paste. Continue to beat until light and fluffy. (Warm almond paste in microwave for 10 seconds).
3. Fold in chocolate.
4. Place 1 tablespoons of almond crumbs in paper cups (muffin cups) or in 2 ounce paper cups. Pack in the ice cream mixture.
5. Sprinkle tops with macaroon/almond cookie crumbs.
6. Freeze until firm. Do not stir. Let stand 5 - 10 minutes before serving.

Jane says, it's not exactly the same as what she remembers from her childhood. But from all her experimentation, it resembles the texture and flavor of her favorite dessert served at Capri's Italian Restaurant. The best!

Cantucci or Biscotti

Oven at 350 degrees
Makes 2 Dozen

Ingredients

1 cup whole, raw almonds
2 cups all-purpose flour
1 1/2 teaspoons baking powder
1/8 teaspoons salt
1/2 teaspoons cinnamon
6 tablespoons butter softened
2/3 cup of confectioners sugar
2 large eggs
1 tablespoon almond extract

Need to buy:
• Raw almonds
• Confectionary sugar
• Almond extract

1. Place the almonds in a preheated 325-degree F. oven and toast the almonds. Cool, and coarsely chop.
2. Mix together the flour, baking powder, cinnamon, and salt. Set aside.
3. In a large bowl, with an electric mixer, beat together the butter and powdered sugar. Add the almonds, the eggs and extract.
5. Add the dry ingredients and continue mixing.
6. On a lightly floured surface, divide the dough in half, and form two loaves about 9 inches long and 2 1/2 inches wide and place on a lightly greased baking sheet.
7. Bake for about 35 minutes or until they are slightly golden brown.
8. Allow to cool for 5 minutes, then using a serrated knife cut into 1/2 inch slices.
9. Place these slices back on the baking sheet, and cook an additional 5-10 minutes or until golden and dry.
10. Store in a cool dry place.

Espresso - You weren't finished with a meal until Grandpa (yes Grandpa) served espresso. To me, this was brown mud that vaguely represented coffee—coffee syrup. Bitter would be a euphemism for what it tasted like---to me! Grandpa would say, "You drink-a this... you get-a hair on you chest." It worked. All my cousins drank espresso and they had plenty of hair...

especially my cousin RoseAnn.

Italian Cassata

Oven at 350 degrees
Serves 10

Ingredients
Cake
1 (18.25 ounce) package pound cake mix
6 tablespoons orange liqueur
1 pint part-skim ricotta cheese
2 tablespoons heavy whipping cream
1/4 cup white sugar
3 tablespoons chopped semisweet chocolate
3 tablespoons candied mixed fruit

Frosting
4 (1 ounce) squares unsweetened chocolate
1/4 cup butter
3 cups confectioners' sugar
1/2 cup hot, strong brewed coffee
1 1/2 teaspoons vanilla extract

Need to buy:
• Pound cake mix
• Heavy cream & ricotta cheese
• Semi-sweet chocolate
• Candied fruit
• Confectionary sugar

1. Prepare the cake mix according to package instructions. Bake in a 9x5 inch loaf pan. Cool completely.
2. With a sharp, serrated knife cut a thin slice from both ends of cooled cake. Cut cake horizontally into 4 even layers. Brush each layer with 1 tablespoon orange liqueur.
3. In medium bowl, beat ricotta cheese with electric mixer until smooth. Beat in cream, sugar, and remaining liqueur. With rubber scraper, fold in chocolate pieces and candied fruits.
4. Place bottom layer of cake on flat plate and spread with one-third of ricotta mix. Place second layer of cake evenly on top of first layer and spread with one-third filling.

Repeat with third layer of cake and filling. Top with remaining cake layer.

5. Gently press loaf into shape. Refrigerate at least 2 hours or until ricotta is firm.

6. To make the frosting: Melt chocolate and butter in top of double boiler, over hot, not boiling, water. Remove from water. Add confectioners' sugar, hot coffee, and vanilla. Beat until smooth. (If too soft to spread, refrigerate until of spreading consistency - about 30 minutes.) Spread frosting over side and top of cake.

7. Refrigerate until serving time.

8. To serve, decorate top with candied fruits, if desired. Or use a pastry tube to decorate the cake with flowers and vines.

Panna Cotta*

Stove top cooking
Serves 4 - 6

Ingredients

1/3 cup skim milk
1 (.25 ounce) envelope
   unflavored gelatin
**2 1/2 cups heavy cream
1/2 cup white sugar
1 1/2 teaspoons vanilla extract

Need to buy:
• Unflavored gelatin
• Heavy cream or
half & half

1. Pour milk into a small bowl, and stir in the gelatin powder. Set aside.
2. In a saucepan, stir together the heavy cream and sugar, and set over medium heat. Bring to a full boil, watching carefully, as the cream will quickly rise to the top of the pan.
3. Pour the gelatin and milk into the cream, stirring until completely dissolved. Cook for one minute, stirring constantly.
4. Remove from heat, and pour into six individual ramekin dishes.
5. Cool the ramekins uncovered at room temperature. When cool, cover with plastic wrap, and refrigerate for at least 4 hours, but preferably overnight before serving.

*NOTE: This is a lovely, soft pudding that goes well with most dishes. It also has no eggs for those of us who can't or don't eat eggs.

**NOTE: I have made this recipe with both heavy cream & half & half. It is much creamier with heavy cream but *perfectly acceptable with the half & half. I have also substituted sugar replacement for real sugar and it just isn't as sweet or good. So use the real sugar... it's only 1/2 cup for the entire recipe.*

The dessert of desserts! A veritable medley of flavors. If you follow this recipe closely, very close-ly; the results will be outstanding. Jane and I once attempted to make Tiramisu and being both cocky and culinary neophytes we assumed we knew what we were doing. Everything was going along fine until we came to the part where you add the mascarpone. Jane didn't know what it was (an Italian cheese) and I was too "macho" to admit I didn't either. I told her, quite confidently, "Oh... that's a sweet Italian wine. So...when the recipe said, "add three cups of mas-carpone (the cheese), since we didn't have real mascarpone "wine" I told her to substitute the mascarpone with three cups of Gallo Rose.

The dessert never rose in the oven. With that amount of alcohol, I'm surprised it didn't blow up the oven. It remained a slushy mixture. We took it out and tasted it. It was yummy; weird but yummy. Essentially, this was a cake you ate with a straw. Ever get drunk on a cake? We did!

MASCARPONE IS A CHEESE!

Tiramisu

Tiramisu literally translates as "pick me up".

No cooking
Serves 4

Ingredients

1 pound mascarpone cheese
at room temperature
1 1/2 cup whipping cream
1 1/4 cup espresso coffee,
cooled
1/2 cup sugar
1/3-cup brandy
24 savoiardi cookies
(ladyfingers) or
Italian sponge cake
dark chocolate, shaved

Need to buy:
• Mascarpone cheese
• Heavy cream
• Brandy
• Italian Ladyfingers
• Dark chocolate

1. Slowly beat in 1/2 cup of sugar to the mascarpone cheese.
2. Whip the cream until soft peaks form, and fold this into the cheese mixture.
3. Add the brandy to the cooled coffee.
4. Carefully dip in ladyfingers one at a time just until the outside of the cookie is barely damp. Arrange cookies side by side in a dish large enough to hold 12 cookies flat.
5. After the first 12 are layered, spread 1/2 of the cheese mixture on top.
6. Sprinkle with enough shaved chocolate to cover lightly, and repeat these layers once more topping the dish with the remaining chocolate.
7. Refrigerate several hours before serving.

Note: Be careful not to over saturate the cookies with the coffee mixture, or you will end up with a runny Tiramisu.

Some basic items needed in a Jewish Kitchen

Vegetables
Celery
Carrots
Onions
Potatoes

Seasonings
Onion powder
Kosher salt
Black pepper

Miscellaneous
Matzo meal
Wide Noodles
Eggs
Prunes
Honey

Oil and Vinegar
Vegetable Oil
White Vinegar
Apple Cider

Utensils
Giant Wooden Spoon
Fry pan

My how the generations have changed. When I went into the kitchen at my Bubbies' (I was allowed in THAT kitchen) I'd watch her create all these wonderful Jewish dishes—from scratch! She'd open a dozen jars with all kinds of stuff—spices, I assumed. For that matter, some of it might have been Pot. Who knew? Who asked? Nothing had labels. A pinch of this, a smidge of that. Everyday things in her kitchen had Yiddish names: A guple (fork) A lefel (spoon) A tup (pot... the cookware) a messer (knife) a gloz (a glass) Tzuker (sugar) Teler (plate) Schmaltz (chicken fat... the Crisco of the Kosher home) Everything worked just fine in Bubbie's kitchen.

She'd say, "Tatella (little one) hand me the messer and a guple. I grew up thinking that a fork was a guple... everywhere. Who knew from the word "fork." Dining out was wonderful. "Excuse me waitress, there's lip-stick on my guple.

My case comes up Tuesday.

MY FATHER'S
JEWISH RECIPES

As a kid, I was never allowed in the kitchen; not because I'd eat anything edible; hence my adult propensity for plumpness, but simply because I was a (as my mother coined it) a "gagootz." That's Italian for: squash... the vegetable not the verb. A squash you might ask? You see, if you called somebody a "gagootz" you were really saying that they were "dumb like a squash."

My problem... accidents in the kitchen. The Jewish side of the family called me a klutz. Different languages, same concept. Either way, I was a mess in the kitchen. Something always spilled, exploded. I always found the salt shaker with the loose top; the five pound bag of flour with the ripped bottom---that was a classic! We had to bring in one of those disaster relief teams to clean that one up. The whole family wheezed and coughed flour for a year. I was once pureeing tomatoes in the blender and forgot to put the top back on... the painters worked out a time payment deal with my parents.

More later...

Jewish Appetizers

In the beginning, God created the appetizer

Baked Salmon
Marinated Veggies
Faux Chopped Liver (Vegetarian)
Hummus & Pita chips
Sweet & Sour Meat Balls

Sheila's Baked Salmon "Gefilte Fish" Loaf

Oven at 350 degrees
Each loaf serves:
6 – 8 appetizers or 4 main course

Ingredients

*2 lbs skinless salmon filets
2 medium onions, chopped
1 grated carrot
1 teaspoon vegetable oil
1 tablespoon sugar or sweetener
1 teaspoon salt
Dash of pepper
2 eggs, beaten
1/2 cup cold water
1/3 cup matzo meal
Parsley, dill, lemon &/or tomato garnish

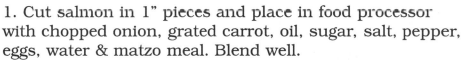

Things to buy:
• Salmon
• Fresh parsley, dill
• Matzo meal

1. Cut salmon in 1" pieces and place in food processor
with chopped onion, grated carrot, oil, sugar, salt, pepper,
eggs, water & matzo meal. Blend well.
2. Spray non-stick coating on 2 Pyrex loaf pans and divide
mixture between them.
3. Bake uncovered 1 hour at 350 degrees.
4. Remove from oven, cool and turn upside down on
platter. Cut into 1/2" slices. Garnish.

NOTE: Make it easy on yourself and ask the butcher to skin
the salmon. It is a messy, smelly job.

Marinated Veggies

Stovetop cooking
4 - 6 servings
Prepare at least 2 days
   before serving

Things to buy:
• Fresh mushrooms,
  Cauliflower

Ingredients

1 pound small fresh mushrooms
  (caps only)
2 cups raw cauliflower
3 carrots, peeled, sliced and par cooked
1 tablespoon vegetable oil
1 tablespoon sugar or Sweetener
3 teaspoon lemon juice or juice of one lemon
  plus the lemon rind
1/4 cup water
1/4 cup white vinegar
3 cloves garlic, halved
1/2 teaspoon salt
Dash pepper, to taste
1/2 teaspoon Italian herbs
2 bay leaves

1. Remove stems from mushrooms. Chop and save for stuffing or other recipes.
2. Cut cauliflower in bite sized pieces.
3. Peel, slice & par cook carrots.
4. Place vegetables in glass bowl (that has a tight cover).
5. Combine remaining ingredients in saucepan. Heat & pour over vegetables.
6. When cool, cover and refrigerate for at least 2 days.
7. Shake jar occasionally (gently).
8. Pour off any liquid and serve with toothpicks.

Marinated Veggies

Ok, this one's really creative and easy to prepare.

I remember this recipe. As a kid, I'd always wonder why Grandma Ida (my Bubbie) never threw out food from the back of the fridge; "depression mentality" I assumed? Nope, she'd create. She'd marinate "old" veggies in her own secret combination of 24 spices and turn them into a veggie-feast. After a little prodding and a promise to give Bubbie top billing for the recipe, we found out she lied... again... there were really only 7 spices and ingredients.

Faux Chopped Liver (Vegetarian Pate)

Stove top cooking
2 cups "liver" spread

Ingredients

3/4 cup of cooked lentils
1 1/2 cups cooked sliced onion
2 tablespoons vegetable oil
   for sautéing
1 1/2 cups green beans, well cooked and
   drained (fresh or canned)
3 hard boiled eggs
1 ounce finely chopped walnuts
1 - 2 teaspoons of sugar/Splenda
20 Tam Tams or other salty crackers
Salt and pepper to taste

Things to buy:
• Lentils
• Green beans
• Walnuts

1. Sauté the onions in the oil over low heat for 20 minutes until limp, translucent and golden. (Do not rush this step).
2. While sautéing onions, cook green beans (or open can), lentils & eggs.
3. Make sure you drain green beans & lentils very well
4. After onions are done, drain as much oil out. I wrap in paper towels and squeeze gently.
5. Combine the sautéed onions with the remaining ingredients in a food processor. Grind until well processed.
6. Season with salt and black pepper.

NOTE: Please make sure you drain green beans, lentils and onions. If you don't drain properly, the mixture becomes very wet and not the right texture. Also, be sure the walnuts are finely chopped

Serve on Ritz or any salty cracker.

Hummus

Buy it or prepare as instructed below

No cooking
Yields about 1 1/2 cups

Ingredients

1 cup chick peas, drained
    (reserve liquid).
    (You can prepare dried chick peas
    or use canned)
1/3 cup tahini (sesame paste)
1 tablespoon roasted garlic
1 tablespoon olive oil
1/4 cup lemon juice (to taste)
Chopped parsley (fresh if available)

Things to buy:
• Chick peas
• Tahini
• Fresh parsley
• Pita bread

1. Place the chick peas, tahini, olive oil, lemon juice and garlic in blender and bend until smooth. Use some reserved liquid if mixture is too stiff.
2. Pile into a small bowl and garnish with parsley leaves. Serve with pita chips (see recipe) or as a dip for vegetables.

Pita Chips

Oven at 350 degrees
Serves 6

Package of whole wheat pita bread
1 egg white
Sesame seeds
1. Cut each pita bread into 4 pieces
2. Dip into egg white
3. Sprinkle with sesame seeds
4. Bake until golden brown and crunchy

According to My Momma, any meatball that's less than a half a pound and doesn't lay on your chest till next Tuesday, is no meatball! Sweet and Sour meatballs are a different species. This is the consummate hot appetizer. Mom usually made about 30 of the spherical delicacies at a time. If I was in the kitchen, only about 20 every made it to the table.

Sweet & Sour Meatballs

Stove top
Serves 6 - 8

Ingredients

1 pound chopped beef, chicken, turkey or combination
1 cup cooked rice
1 egg
2 tablespoons catsup
1 teaspoon each garlic & onion powder
Salt & pepper to taste

Sauce

1 cup tomato catsup or 1 cup taco sauce
1 cup grape jelly
1/4 cup red wine vinegar

1. Mix first 6 ingredients together & make small meatballs (one inch).
2. Combine sauce mixture together & heat in a saucepan until jelly has melted.
3. Place meatballs in sauce & cook 25 minutes.
4. Place onto serving dish & serve warm with toothpicks.

Things to buy:
• Chopped beef, turkey or chicken

Always a surprise and always delicious. My Aunt would embellish her pea soup with anything from hot-dogs to flanken... that's a Jewish type of brisket that most gourmets consider a waste product from the slaughter house. But in the hands of Aunt Sophie, the flanken in her pea soup became "the prize at the bottom of the Cracker-Jacks box." Just two bites of her flanken and you understood the concept of gastric reflux. So, stay away from the flankin and just make the soup.

You'll love it.

Jewish Soups

You'll never miss Campbell's again

Healthy Fish Chowder
Low-Fat Matzo Balls with Broth
Mushroom Barley
Pea Soup
Sweet & Sour Cabbage Soup

Healthy Fish Chowder

Stove top cooking
Serves 6

Ingredients

1 carrot peeled & diced
1 onion, chopped
1 cup celery, diced
1 leek, peeled & sliced
3 potatoes, peeled & diced
1 cup tomato puree
2 vegetable bullions
1 teaspoon thyme
1 teaspoon oregano
1 teaspoon salt
1 teaspoon sour salt
6 cups water
1 tablespoon olive oil
1 pound boneless fish fillets, diced, (carp, whitefish, pike flounder)
Tabasco sauce (to taste)

Things to buy:
• Leek
• Boneless fish
• Canned tomato puree
• Sour salt

1. Prepare vegetables and sauté in 1 tablespoon olive oil for 5 minutes.
2. Add tomato puree, water, bullion and herbs. Cover & simmer for 1 hour until vegetables are tender.
3. Add fish & simmer 15 minutes.
4. Season to taste with tabasco and add seasoning to taste.
5. Serve piping hot.

Serve with crunchy bread for a delicious light summer meal.

Low-fat Matzo Balls in Chicken Soup

Stove top cooking
10 matzo balls
3 cups chicken broth

Ingredients for Matzo Balls

1/2 cup matzo meal
4 egg whites, slightly beaten
2 tablespoons vegetable canola oil
2 tablespoons water
1/4 teaspoon salt

Things to buy:
• Matzo meal
• Chicken broth

1. Combine all ingredients and put into refrigerator for 20 minutes.
2. Shape into 10 balls.
3. Boil in 3 cups hot chicken soup or chicken bullion for 20 minutes.
4. They may be made ahead and reheated.

Note 1: These are low fat because we are not using the egg yolk (which has all the fat) in the matzo balls.
Note 2: For firmer matzo balls increase the amount of matzo meal. For softer balls, increase the number of egg whites. For the softest balls, use stiffly beaten egg whites.

Ingredients for Chicken Soup

1. You can either make homemade chicken broth OR
2. Use cans of chicken broth. "Doctoring" the canned soup is easy. Just add chopped carrots, celery & a bay leaf and simmer for an hour. You can either leave the vegetables (take out the bay leaf) in or if you are a purist take all the veggies out.
3. Add the matzo balls to the broth and serve with chopped parsley on top.

Wow I really loved these matzo balls. Mom, made them with an Italian flair… lots of pepper. She once tried making them with oregano; my father considered this an act of international terrorism and financial sanctions were initiated. Also watch the amount of water you use; too much and you wind up with matzo-sludge; too little and you got matzo-gummies.
So, follow this simple recipe carefully and you'll make "perfect" matzo balls each and every time.

Mushroom Barley Soup

Stove top cooking
Serves 6 – 8

Ingredients

2 medium onions chopped
3 cloves chopped garlic
1 ounce dried mushrooms
16 ounces button mushrooms
    (try a variety)
1 cup whole barley (not instant)
1 quart water
1 quart beef bullion, beef broth
1 bay leaf
Salt to taste
2 teaspoons canola or olive oil
1/2 teaspoon ground white pepper to taste
Chopped parsley

Things to buy:
• Dried mushrooms,
  button mushrooms
• Barley
• Beef bullion
• Fresh parsley

1. Sauté onions and garlic in oil until limp
(about 5 minutes).
2. Add cup of barley.
3. Add liquids, bay leaf.
4. Cover and cook on low/med head (it should be a slow
boil) for 1 hour.
5. While soup is cooking soak dried mushrooms.
6. After 1 hour of cooking the barley, and mushrooms
(chop reconstituted and button/variety).
7. Cook an additional 30 minutes.
8. Use a hand processor to make soup fairly smooth (as
smooth as you like). Steve hates lumps.
9. Season with salt & pepper to taste.
10. To improve flavor, refrigerate overnight. Reheat. When
serving, sprinkle parsley on top.

Pea Soup

Stove top cooking
Serves 6 – 8

Ingredients

2 stalks celery chopped
3 cloves garlic chopped
2 onions chopped
2 carrots, sliced
1 bag 10 ounce dried green peas
1 quart water
1 quart beef bullion, beef broth
salt & pepper, to taste

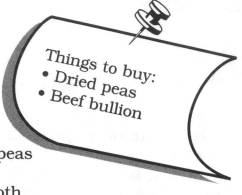

Things to buy:
• Dried peas
• Beef bullion

1. Sauté celery, onions, garlic, & carrots until limp (about 5 minutes).
2. Add bag of dried peas (wash & pick through before adding to pot).
3. Add liquids.
4. Cover and cook on low/med head (it should be a slow boil) for 1 1/2 hours.
5. Season to taste.
6. Use a hand processor to puree the soup. It should be a fairly smooth consistency.
7. You can add a cooked frankfurter or chopped ham to each bowl for a more filling soup.

Make the day before and reheat. Serve with pumpernickel, rye bread or pita crisps (see recipe)

Once again... as a kid I really didn't like cabbage soup... but as a kid, my idea of fine dining was Oscar Meyer Bologna and M&Ms... no peanuts! I did have a somewhat refined palate back then.
When Grandma made this soup, the aromas permeated the neighborhood. People would follow the fragrance right back to the kitchen window. And the fragrance of the soup was only surpassed by its taste. Grandma would cook enough to feed the entire extended family of 12 three times over. One caveat, after 12 people, in one small room, finished a bowl of Grandma's Sweet and Sour Cabbage soup and then had seconds... Well, there were other aromas and fragrances we all had to contend with.

But, as usual, everyone blamed the dog.

Sweet & Sour Cabbage Soup

Stove top cooking
Serves 6 – 8

Ingredients

2 onions chopped
2 potatoes chopped
2 stalks celery chopped
3 carrots chopped
2 pounds cabbage chopped or shredded
1 can 68 ounce chopped tomatoes plus 1 can water
2 quarts liquid (water, beef bullion, beef broth or combination)
1 teaspoon salt
1/2 teaspoon white pepper
1/4 cup lemon juice or apple cider vinegar to taste
2 – 3 tablespoons brown or white sugar (you can use splenda – it comes in a brown sugar substitute). I like brown sugar best in this recipe.

Things to buy:
• Cabbage
• Can chopped tomatoes
• Brown sugar

1. Sauté onions, potatoes, celery, carrots until limp (about 5 minutes).
2. Add cabbage and sauté 5 more minutes.
3. Add tomatoes, liquid and cook about 1 hour.
4. After cooked, season with salt, pepper, lemon or vinegar, and sugar to taste.
5. If you like a more processed soup, you can run it through the food processor, but not too much.
6. If you like sour cream (or yogurt), you can add a dollop to each bowl before serving.

Better if you make the day before and reheat.

Here's where Jane and I disagree.
I did a survey. I interviewed 10 Jews over
the age of 50. When they were growing
up... NOT ONE OF THEM WAS EVER
SERVED A SALAD BEFORE A MEAL!...
NOT ONE.
It just wasn't done. To my father
(conservative Jewish) salad was rabbit
food. To my Grandma Ida, salad was any-
thing that wasn't meat. In her mentality,
vegetarians were moments away from
starvation and death. Now, that's not to
say that Jane's salad creations are not
delicious; they are. But Jewish? I'm not so
sure. When I was growing up, the only
"salads" we ever had at Grandma's started
with the name..."Green Giant."

Jewish Salads

You won't need your can-opener for these

Carrot Salad
Chopped Salad with Goat Cheese & Mandarin Oranges
Crunchy Cauliflower & Pea Salad
Cucumber with Yogurt Dressing
Health Salad

Carrot Salad

No cooking
Serves 4

Ingredients

4 carrots peeled & grated
handful of raisins
1/4 cup fresh orange juice
1/2 teaspoon sugar
   (white or brown) to taste
1/2 teaspoon cinnamon (optional)
1/4 cup pignoli nuts or sliced almonds
   (optional)

Things to buy:
• Raisins
• Orange juice
• Pine nuts or
   sliced almonds

1. Peel and grate carrots.
2. Add raisins, orange juice & add sugar to taste.
3. Mix and put in refrigerator until ready.

Great with roasted chicken or fish.

*Chopped salad with goat cheese & mandarin oranges
Ok, this doesn't sound like a typical Jewish dish. I
guess you're raising an eyebrow because the word
"goat" and "cheese" are in the same title... you know,
meat and milk together... very NOT Kosher. Read again,
it's just Goat cheese, no goat.*

*I checked with the entire Jewish side of my family. No
one has ever used goat cheese. It seems Jane came up
with this wonderful mix of flavors and textures and
CLAIMED it was a Jewish delight. Jewish it's probably
not, a delight... it definitely is.*

Chopped Salad with Goat Cheese & Mandarin Oranges

No cooking
Serves 4 - 6

Ingredients

1/4 head cabbage, chopped
1 medium head romaine
  lettuce, chopped
2 carrots, peeled & chopped
1 cucumber, peeled, seeded
  & chopped
20 grape tomatoes cut in half
1/2 cup scallions, chopped
  (use both white & green parts)
1/2 each red, green &
  yellow pepper,
  seeded & chopped
2 stalks celery, chopped
1 small can mandarin oranges, drained (save liquid)
1/2 cup goat cheese in small pieces
4 ounces slivered almonds

Dressing recipe on next page

Things to buy:
• Cabbage, romaine lettuce, cucumber, grape tomatoes, scallions, red, green & yellow peppers
• Mandarin oranges
• Goat cheese
• Slivered almonds

1. Chop all ingredients to approximately same size
& combine in mixing bowl.
2. Mix the dressing or use prepared vinaigrette.
3. Add dressing to chopped vegetables. Toss in
mandarin oranges & goat cheese.
4. Garnish with slivered almonds.
5. Serve immediately.

Dressing (Make or use store-bought olive oil-based vinaigrette)
2 tablespoons each -olive oil and safflower oil
1/4 cup red wine vinegar
1/4 cup mandarin orange liquid
2 tablespoons sugar or sugar substitute
Salt & pepper to taste
1/4 teaspoon each of onion powder & garlic powder

Crunchy Cauliflower & Pea Salad

No cooking
Serves 6 - 8

Ingredients

1 1/4 cup chopped
   fresh cauliflower
1 - 10 ounce package
   frozen peas, thawed
1 1/4 cup diced celery
1/2 red pepper, seeded
   and diced
1/2 cup diced scallions
1/2 cup nonfat sour cream
3/4 cup ranch-style dressing
1/2 teaspoon white pepper
3 tablespoons red wine vinegar
1/2 cup chopped fresh parsley
1/2 cup chopped toasted almonds, for garnish

Things to buy:
• Chopped fresh cauliflower
• Frozen peas
• Red pepper, scallions
• Non-fat sour cream or yogurt
• Ranch-style dressing
• Fresh parsley
• Chopped almonds

1. Chop cauliflower in small pieces & mix with peas, celery, diced pepper and scallions.
2. Combine the sour cream or yogurt with dressing in a separate bowl. Add all the spices, vinegar to the dressing and add to the vegetables.
3. Toss and chill.
4. Garnish with almonds just before serving.

Cucumbers with Yogurt Dressing

No cooking
Serves 6

Ingredients

3 cucumbers – peeled, seeded
   & thinly sliced
1 medium onion finely chopped
1 cup plain yogurt
2 teaspoons sugar or Splenda
2 garlic cloves minced
1/2 cup white vinegar
1/4 cup water
1/4 teaspoon salt
White pepper to taste
Chopped parsley & dill

Things to buy:
• Cucumber
• Yogurt
• Fresh parsley
  & dill

1. Combine cucumbers & onions in a glass container that has a snugly fit lid.
2. Mix garlic, vinegar, water, sweetener, salt & pepper together.
3. Pour over cucumbers & mix to coat evenly.
4. Refrigerate overnight.
5. Mix before serving.
6. Garnish with parsley & dill.

Health Salad

No cooking
Serves 4 – 6

Ingredients

1/2 medium cabbage, chopped
1 medium onion chopped
2 carrots, chopped
1/2 each green and red pepper,
    seeded & chopped
1 cucumber, peeled, seeded & chopped
1 cup white vinegar
1/2 cup water
4 tablespoons sugar or sweetener
2 tablespoons vegetable oil
Salt & pepper to taste

1. Chop all vegetables to approximately same size.
2. Combine vinegar, water, sweetener oil and herbs.
3. Mix together and place in refrigerator until ready to serve.

Things to buy:
• Cabbage, green &
red pepper &
cucumber

My Grandmother would buy inexpensive cuts of meat from our butcher. He'd hold them aside for her to pick up just prior to them being sent off to the dog-food factory. She would cut it up, beat it up, pull off the delicious strands of fats, grizzle and sinew, then marinate the meats in her own special ingredients and cook them to perfection. No body ever asked "what part of the cow was this from?" The brown sauce that covered the meat usually hid its cosmetic imperfections and it always tasted fine. We kept quiet... we were young but not stupid and besides... Grandma's wooden spoon had multiple uses.

Jewish Entrees

Let the games begin

Brisket
Honey-Orange Chicken
Honey-Apple Glazed turkey Breast
Salmon Croquettes
Sautéed Red Snapper with Lemon Asparagus Puree

Brisket

Stove top or Oven cooking – 450 degrees
Serves 6 - 8

Ingredients

Version 1

1 - 5 pound brisket. I use the flat cut which is leaner and has less grizzle. You can also use shoulder roast of beef, chuck or end of steak.
3 tablespoons flour
2 garlic cloves. peeled & minced
2 tablespoons vegetable oil
2 cups water
3 onions, peeled & diced
2 stalks celery, chopped
6 to 8 carrots, peeled & sliced on the diagonal
1 package onion soup mix

Version 2
salt & pepper
2 cloves of garlic, peeled & cut in half
3 tablespoons flour
3 onions, peeled & diced
1 - 14 1/2 ounce can of tomatoes (I prefer chopped)
2 stalks celery, chopped
6 to 8 carrots, peeled and sliced on the diagonal
1/2 can water
1/2 cup red wine
1/4 cup chopped parsley
1 teaspoon thyme
3 small bay leaves
1 sprig rosemary

Things to buy:
• Brisket
• Onion soup mix
• Can chopped tomatoes

Version 1   The easy way

1. Dredge meat in flour then brown in the oil.
2. Add the garlic & onions around the meat & sauté until limp.
3. Add the onion soup mix & water. Simmer on top of the stove for 1 hour.
4. Add the carrots & celery after 1 hour.
5. Continue cooking on the stove about 2 hours more or until tender.

Version 2   Not as easy

1. Sprinkle salt & pepper over the brisket & rub with garlic. Dredge meat in flour.
2. Sear the brisket in the oil and place fat side up in a large casserole. Sprinkle onions on top & sides of the meat.
3. Cover with tomatoes, red wine, water, bay leaf, thyme & rosemary.
4. Cover & bake in a preheated 325 degree oven for about 3 hours. Baste with juices.
5. Add parsley, celery, carrots & bake, uncovered, for about 30 minutes more until carrots are cooked.

In both cases, it is best to cook a day or two ahead. This way, you can skim the fat from the surface before reheating. Cut the brisket on a cutting board. Look for the grain and cut across it. Serve with farfel (boiled egg barley noodles), noodle kugel or potato pancakes.

Honey-Orange Baked Chicken

Stove top cooking & Oven at 325 degrees
Serves 4 - 6

Ingredients
Cut chicken in eighths (3 – 4 pounds)
2 eggs or egg substitute
2 teaspoons water
1 cup matzo meal
1 teaspoon salt
1/8 teaspoon black pepper
1/4 cup vegetable oil
1 cup hot water
1/4 cup honey
1 cup orange juice
3/4 teaspoon ground ginger

Things to buy:
• Chicken
• Honey
• Orange juice
• Ground ginger

1. Beat the eggs with the 2 teaspoons water.
2. Mix matzo meal with salt & pepper.
3. Dip chicken in the egg, then matzo meal.
4. Heat oil on medium high and brown chicken on all sides.
5. Preheat oven to 325 degrees.
6. Combine hot water, honey & orange juice.
7. Place chicken in casserole; pour honey mixture over cooking chicken. Add ginger.
8. Cover & cook for 45 minutes to 1 hour, basting occasionally.
9. Garnish with orange slices.

Honey-Apple Glazed Turkey Breast

Oven 325 degrees
Serves 6 – 8

Ingredients

1/3 cup honey
1 tablespoon dry mustard
1 (6-1/2 to 7 pound) turkey breast, skin and all visible fat removed
1 6 ounce can frozen apple juice concentrate, thawed and undiluted

1. Combine honey, mustard and apple juice in a bowl, stirring well. Set aside.
2. Place turkey breast in roasting pan, insert meat thermometer into meaty portion so that it does not touch the bone. Baste with honey mixture.
3. Cover and bake at 325 degrees Fahrenheit for 1 hour. Uncover and bake an additional hour or until meat thermometer registers 170 degrees, basting frequently with the honey sauce mixture that accumulates in pan. (Total baking time is approximately 2 hours, ovens may vary).
4. Let cool at least 15-20 minutes before slicing.

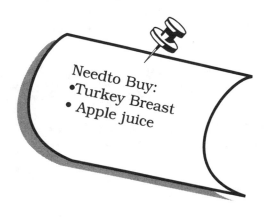

Need to Buy:
•Turkey Breast
• Apple juice

Salmon Croquettes with dill

Oven cooking – 400 degrees
Makes 8 croquettes – serves 4

Ingredients

2 slices white bread
1 1/2 pounds boneless,
    skinless salmon fillet*
4 scallions, finely chopped
2 tablespoons chopped fresh dill
2 tablespoons finely chopped fresh parsley
1 clove garlic, minced
1/2 teaspoon freshly grated lemon rind
1/2 cup egg substitute or 1 egg & 2 egg whites
Salt & freshly ground pepper

Things to buy:
• Salmon
• Scallions
• Fresh parsley, dill

1. Lightly spray a nonstick baking sheet with spray oil. Place the baking sheet in the oven and preheat to 400 degrees.
2. Soak bread in warm water for 3 minutes. Squeeze the bread in your fingers to wring out the excess liquid. Place the bread in a mixing bowl.
3. Finely chop the salmon. In the old day you would chop by hand or use a handcrank meat grinder. Today we use a food processor. First, cut the salmon into 1-inch pieces before chopping. Run the processor in short burst. Don't over process or you'll wind up with a spongy puree.
4. Transfer the salmon to the mixing bowl with the bread. Stir in the scallions, dill, parsley, garlic, lemon peel, egg, & salt & pepper to taste.
5. Wet your hands and form the salmon mixture into 8 3-inch balls.Gently flattening each with the palm of your hand. Lightly spray the tops of the croquettes with oil.

6. Bake the salmon croquettes until lightly browned and firm (10 to 15 minutes) turning the croquettes after 5 minutes

7. Serve at once.

Don't forget to have the butcher skin the salmon.

Salmon Croquettes

Thursday was Salmon croquette day. I dreaded Thursdays. "Salmon! Salmon again? Mom didn't you read that they found out that Salmon is poisonous to small kids?" After a few choice words (mostly in Italian) I realized that it would be beneficial for me to immediately run out of the kitchen before she made Steve croquettes.
As a kid, I hated Salmon Croquettes.
As an adult, I can't believe
what a schmuck I was...

These are delicious and easy to make.

Sautéed Red Snapper Fillets with Lemon Asparagus Puree

Stove top
4 servings

Ingredients

1 1/2 pound asparagus,
    trimmed
1 large boiling potato
    (about 1 pound)
four 6-ounce red snapper fillets with skin
2 teaspoons olive oil
2 teaspoons fresh lemon juice, or to taste

Things to buy:
• Asparagus
• Red snapper

1. Cut tips off 12 asparagus spears and reserve. Cut all spears into 1/2-inch pieces and cook in a saucepan of salted boiling water until tender, about 6 minutes.
2. Transfer cooked asparagus with a slotted spoon to a blender and purée with 1 cup cooking liquid, reserving remaining cooking liquid in pan. Keep purée warm in a small saucepan.
3. Have ready a bowl of ice and cold water. Return reserved cooking liquid to a boil and blanch reserved asparagus tips until just tender, about 3 minutes. Drain tips and immediately transfer to ice water to stop cooking. Drain tips and reserve for garnish.
4. Scrub potato and cut lengthwise into four 1/2-inch-thick slices. In saucepan cook potato slices in salted boiling water to cover until tender, about 5-10 minutes, and transfer with a slotted spoon to a bowl. Keep potatoes warm, covered.
5. Pat snapper dry and season with salt and pepper. In a large non-stick skillet heat oil over moderate heat until hot but not smoking and cook fish, skin sides down, about 3 minutes, or until skin is golden brown. Turn fish over and

cook 2 minutes more, or until just cooked through.

6. Whisk lemon juice and salt and pepper to taste into asparagus purée. Spoon some sauce onto 4 plates and top each portion with a potato slice and a fish fillet.

7. Garnish fish with asparagus tips and serve remaining sauce on side.

VEGGIES???

Who knew from Veggies? Growing up in two kitchens I soon realized that Italians worked with three vegetables: Tomatoes, Onions and Mushrooms; occasionally Grandma Angelina would introduce hot peppers which introduced us to Tums. Grandma Ida worked with dozens of vegetables... all potatoes. Potatoes were THEE vegetable. Boiled, Baked, Roasted --I liked the crispies... I always liked the crispies, deep fried in the roasting pan... when I was 42, they took out my gall bladder.

I'll have the BAKED potato, please.

Jewish Vegetables

Even baby cousin Moisha's gonna love these... and he hates everything!

Creamed Spinach
Grilled Veggies
Vegetable Cutlets
Tzimmes
Vegetable Roll

Creamed Spinach

Stove top
Serves 6

Ingredients

2 pounds fresh spinach or
    2 packages frozen
    chopped spinach

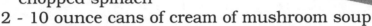

Things to buy:
• Frozen or fresh spinach
• Mushroom soup
• Chinese noodles

2 - 10 ounce cans of cream of mushroom soup
1/2 teaspoon each of onion & garlic powder
1/2 can of water or chicken bullion
Chinese noodles

1. Steam fresh spinach until limp (about 3 minutes) or
steam the frozen spinach until cooked (about 8 minutes).
2. Drain spinach until almost dry.
3. Combine soup, onion, garlic & liquid together.
4. Mix in the spinach. Cook until completely heated.
5. Sprinkle Chinese noodles on top. Serve immediately.

Grilled Veggies

Oven or Barbeque cooking
Serves 6

Ingredients

1 onion (sweet), sliced
1 white & 1 sweet potato,
   peeled & sliced
2 sliced portobello mushrooms,
   sliced
2 medium green zucchini, peeled
   & cut in strips
1 small eggplant (Italian is best) & peeled & sliced
1 red & 1 green pepper seeded & sliced
Bunch of thin asparagus, ends cut off
Use any other veggie or combination that you like...slice or
cut in thin strips
1/4 - 1/2 cup olive oil or olive oil & safflower oil mixed in
equal parts
1/2 teaspoon each of garlic powder, onion powder,
paprika, basil, oregano, thyme, white pepper
2 teaspoons salt

Things to buy:
• Sweet onions, white
  & sweet potato,
• Portobello mush-
  rooms, zucchini,
  eggplant, red &
  green peppers,
  asparagus

1. Prepare vegetables and place into large baggies.
2. Mix oil & herbs together & pour over vegetables. Mix
well.
3. Place seasoned vegetables on cookie sheets. Keep them
in single layer.
4. Preheat oven to 450 degrees. Place trays in oven and
cook about 10 -12 minutes. You want the vegetables to be
browned. Be careful opening oven door. Very Hot Steam!
5. Serve hot or cold.

Vegetable Cutlets

Stove top
Oven cooking 400 degrees
Makes 12 – 15 Cutlets

Things to buy:
• Potatoes, onions, mushrooms
• Matzo meal
• Canned carrots, green bean, peas

Ingredients

6 medium potatoes, peeled and
  cut into 2-inch cubes
Butter spray
1 tablespoon vegetable oil
2 medium onions, chopped
6 mushrooms, chopped
1 (14 1/2 ounce) can diced carrots, drained (NOTE 1)
1 (14 1/2 ounce) can cut green beans, drained
1 (14 1/2 ounce) can peas, drained
2 eggs or egg subsitute
2 cups matzo meal (approximately)
Salt, freshly ground pepper, 1/2 teaspoon each, garlic &
onion powder

1. Preheat oven to 400 degrees
2. Cook potatoes in boiling salted water for 20 minutes, or
until tender. Mash.
3. In a skillet, heat butter and sauté onions and mushrooms until tender. Pour mushroom mixture into a bowl
with mashed potatoes. Stir in carrots, green beans, peas
and 2 eggs. Blend thoroughly.
4. Add enough matzo meal so that mixture can be shaped
into large patties. Season with salt and pepper.
5. Shape into 12 to 15 patties. Spray patties with butter
spray. Place on a well-sprayed cookie sheet.
6. Bake for 45 minutes at 400 degrees, or until lightly
golden browned. Turn after 20 minutes.
7. Serve hot with your favorite mushroom gravy or serve
with low fat sour cream. Delicious!

Tzimmes

Oven 350 degree
Serves 10 – 12 side servings

Ingredients

3 pounds carrots, peeled & sliced diagonally into 1-inch pieces
2 pounds yams, peeled & sliced into 2 inch circles
16 large pitted prunes, cut into thirds
1/2 to 2/3 cup honey
1 tablespoon ground cinnamon
Freshly grated nutmeg to taste

1. Preheat oven to 350 degrees. Coat a large covered casserole with vegetable cooking spray.
2. Layer the carrots, yams & prunes alternately in the prepared pan, drizzling with honey to taste and sprinkling with the spices.
3. Add water to cover the ingredients. Cover & bake 30 minutes.
4. Uncover & bake 30 additional minutes, or until the carrots & yams are soft & the liquid is reduced to a thick & slightly sticky consistency.

Things to buy:
• Yams
• Pitted prunes
• Honey
• Nutmeg

Vegetable Roll

Stove top cooking
Oven cooking 425 degrees
Serves 6

Things to buy:
• Canned mushrooms
• Frozen or fresh spinach
• Puff pastry sheet

Ingredients

2 small onions, diced
1 4ounce can mushrooms or
   use fresh button mushrooms sliced & sautéed
1 10 ounce box frozen, chopped spinach or use one bag
of fresh spinach, cleaned & sautéed
1 puff pastry sheet
Salt & pepper, to taste
Dab of margarine, 1 tablespoon olive oil
Seasoned breadcrumbs
1 egg, beaten

1. Cook spinach in 1 tablespoon of water.
2. While cooking spinach, sauté onions & mushrooms in
olive oil.
3. Roll out pastry sheet. Rub margarine on the inside of
pastry sheet.
4. Combine spinach, onions & mushrooms. Add salt &
pepper to taste. Remove as mush water from vegetables.
5. Sprinkle bread crumbs over pastry sheet.
6. Place vegetable mixture over bread crumbs, spread
evenly.
7. Roll up jellyroll style.
8. Brush egg on top.
9. Bake at 425 degrees F for 20 to 30 minutes, until
golden brown on top.

Jewish Starches

Cellulite, the Yiddish word for Pudding

Kasha Varnishkas
Challah Bread Pudding
Crispy Fried Potato Latkes
Noodle Pudding
Sweet Potato Kugel

(pronounced: LOT-KISS)

Home fries? Nope? McDonald's hash browns? .....well almost—but better.

I loved these before I was born. Potato + Onion + Chicken fat (ok, leave out the chicken fat) = LOVE! Follow this classic recipe (Jane was strictly forbidden to modify this with threats of being disowned by the family) Fry-em up nice and crispy, drain and serve. Wait till the pan cools before picking away at those munchy morsels left in the pan. Serve with sour cream or apple sauce. I liked them with apple sauce. I only ate sour cream with rye-bread ends... but that's another story.

Kasha Varnishkas (Bow tie pasta & Mushrooms)

Stove top cooking
Serves 4 - 6

Ingredients

1 cup Kasha
   (buckwheat groats)
2 cups small bow tie noodles
Salt, to taste
1 tablespoon extra-virgin olive oil or vegetable oil
1 medium onion, peeled & finely chopped
1 1/2 cups thinly sliced button mushrooms, shitakes or
fresh porcini
1 egg white
2 cups beef or chicken broth or water
Freshly ground black pepper

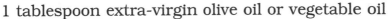

Things to buy:
• Kasha
• Bow tie noodles
• Button mushrooms
• Beef or chicken broth

1. Wash the kasha under cold water. Drain & blot dry.
2. Cook bow ties in boiling salted water until al dente (6 –
8 minutes). Drain, refresh under cold water & drain again.
3. Heat the oil in a large, heavy saucepan. Add onions &
mushrooms & cook over medium heat until onions are
golden brown & mushrooms have lost most of their liquid
(5 – 7 minutes).
4. Put cooked onions & mushrooms in a bowl to let cool.
5. Add the kasha & egg white to the pan and stir well.
Cook over high heat, stirring for 1 – 2 minutes until the
kasha grains are dry.
6. Stir in the onion, mushroom, broth, salt & pepper.
7. Simmer the kasha, covered until tender & all the liquid
is absorbed (about 15 minutes).
8. Add the bow ties the last 3 minutes. Season to taste.

Challah Bread Pudding

Oven at 325 degrees
12 servings

Ingredients

2 1/2 cups 2% low-fat milk
1/2 cup dried tart cherries
1/2 cup golden raisins
1/2 cup fat-free sweetened
   condensed milk
2 teaspoons vanilla extract
1 teaspoon ground cinnamon
1/2 teaspoon freshly grated nutmeg
1/4 teaspoon salt
3 large eggs
8 cups (1-inch) cubes challah or other
   egg bread (1/2 loaf)
Cooking spray
2 tablespoons sugar

Things to buy:
• Dried tart cherries
• Golden raisins
• Fat-free condensed milk
• Nutmeg
• Challah

1. Preheat oven to 325°.
2. Combine the first 9 ingredients in a large bowl.
3. Add challah cubes, tossing to coat. Let challah mixture stand 30 minutes, stirring occasionally.
4. Coat an 11 x 7-inch baking dish with cooking spray.
5. Spoon the challah mixture into dish, and sprinkle with sugar.
6. Bake at 325° for 55 minutes or until pudding is set. Let pudding stand 15 minutes before serving.

Crisp Fried Potato Latkes

Stovetop
10 Servings

Ingredients

2 1/2 pounds potatoes;
  peeled
1 large onion
3 large eggs; lightly beaten
1 teaspoon salt; or to taste
1/8 teaspoon black pepper, fresh ground or to taste
1/4 cup Matzo meal or 2 tablespoon all-purpose flour

Things to buy:
• Matzo meal
• Potatoes or other vegetables (zucchini, sweet potato)

1. Shred or grate the potatoes alternately with the onion to keep the potatoes from darkening. (The size of the shreds is a matter of personal taste.) Coarse shreds produce lacier latkes with rough edges. Fine shreds or grated potatoes produce denser, smoother latkes.)
2. Squeeze the excess liquid from potato and onion shreds.
3. Mix in the eggs, salt, pepper and matzo meal (or flour). Let the mixture rest for about 5 mins., so that the matzo meal can absorb some moisture. If the mixture still seems very wet, add a bit more matzo meal.
4. In a very large skillet, over medium-high heat, heat oil that is about 1/8-1/4" deep until it is very hot but not smoking.
5. Use a large spoon to transfer some of the potato mixture to the oil; then flatten the mixture slightly with the back of a spoon. The latkes will be irregularly shaped. Fry the latkes until they are well browned on both sides and crisp around the edges.
6. Drain them well on paper towels.
7. Accompany with applesauce, sour cream, and/or yogurt, as desired.

Ruth's Simple Noodle Kugel (Pudding)

Oven at 350 degrees
Serves 8

Ingredients

8 ounces extra wide noodles
8 ounces container low fat
  sour cream
8 ounces low fat cottage cheese
3/4 cup sugar or Splenda equivalent
1 - 2 teaspoons vanilla (depends how
  much you like vanilla)
1 cup raisans soaked in water
4 eggs or egg substitute
1 cup low fat milk
1 teaspoon butter flavor (optional)
1/2 teaspoon cinnamon
1/2 cup cornflakes

Things to buy:
• Extra wide noodles
• Sour cream
• Cottage cheese
• Cornflakes

1. Grease baking dish and soak raisins in warm water
2. Cook noodles until al dente. Drain.
3. Add sour cream, cottage cheese, sugar/Splenda, vanilla,
butter flavor & raisins to cooked noodles.
4. Beat eggs and pour eggs and milk into noodle mixture
5. Spread into baking dish.
6. Sprinkle with cinnamon & cornflakes.
7. Bake for 30 - 45 minutes until browned.

*NOTE: You can add drained pineapple, mandarin oranges,
apples, pears or any combination to this basic mixture. Be
creative. I've even added chocolate bits and nuts. The
combinations all depend upon if this dish is to be served
with the main course or for dessert.*

NOTE 2: Leftovers are best if heated before serving.

Noodle Pudding

Is this dessert? Is this a side dish... Side dish? Never! Calling a noodle pudding (AKA koogle) a side dish is like saying you may get moist from a tidal wave. To paraphrase Sarah Lee: "Nobody doesn't like noodle pudding" Remember it's not just a Jewish dish. The Italian side of my family loved it too "cept they never called it "koogle"; they always tried to find an Italian name for it... "Crispy sweet fettuccini" " Noodles-Napoli" They all ate it. They all loved it.

You will too.

Sweet Potato Kugel

Oven at 375 degrees
Serves 12

Ingredients

6 small sweet potatoes, peeled and grated
3 apples, peeled and grated
1 cup raisins
1 cup matzo meal
2 tsp cinnamon
1 cup fruit juice or water

1. Preheat oven to 375 degrees.
2. Mix ingredients together.
3. Press into large baking dish.
4. Bake 45 minutes at 375 degrees until crisp on top.

Things to buy:
• Sweet potatoes
• Apples
• Raisins
• Matzo meal

Jewish Desserts

Did you call your mother today?
Ok, you can have dessert

Compote
Hamantaschen
Festival Fruit Strudel
Honey Cake
Peach or Plum Kuchen

The Case of the Deadly Bunt Cake

*People who go through a divorce are always asked.
"What happened" "When did you notice things falling
apart with you two?" Few of us know the day, the straw
that broke the camel's back...
I know the day and time exactly.
After being banned from kitchens most of my adoles-
cent life for the crime of Excessive Messiness, And, after
marrying a lady whose sole purpose in life was to clean
and be tidy—you can see my predicament. Since I was
used to being banished from Kitchens, I took no offense
when my new bride followed in my mother's footsteps.
My reputation preceded me.
I was watching TV one Sunday afternoon when I
heard this strange grunting sound coming from my no-
man's land... AKA the kitchen. "Honey" I asked.
"Are you ok?"
My wife screamed back. "I can't get this bunt cake out
of the pan. I have to serve it at a meeting in an hour...
grunt, grunt, crap, grunt." I said, "Do you need some
help in there?"
My wife, still screaming; "This is a double chocolate,
fudge filled bunt cake... we have a white kitchen... are
you out of your mind? Grunt, shit, grunt" I peeked into
the kitchen and watched her struggle, trying desperately
to loosen the cake from the pan with spatulas, knives,
wooden spoons. "Are you sure I can't help?" I said
sheepishly.
She looked up. "Ok" she said, "come in here. BUT... if
you get one crumb the counters, the floor... anyplace...
I'll kill you.
I surveyed the bunt cake, analyzing each chocolate
morsel's position with respect to the pan. "Where's the
serving plate that the cake will be served on..." I asked.*

"Here, it's my grandmother's. It's an antique, be careful", She said. I moved over a small step stool so I could be about a foot or two above the counter. I turned over the double chocolate, fudge filled cake directly above the serving plate so as to catch all the crumbs. I figured Newton's second law of motion... momentum, should come into play. I assumed that if I shook and jerked the cake just right..., gravity would do the rest. It worked perfectly. I shook and jerked and the double chocolate and low and behold the fudge filled bunt cake came right out!

One small problem. I was too high. The 2 pound cake was about two feet from the plate when it left the pan. And, building up speed (thanks to gravity) it smashed down onto Grandma's antique serving plate shattering it into thousands of small shards of porcelain. Oh but there's more... the double chocolate, fudge filled bunt cake then struck the counter with the impact of a meteor splitting open the cake and allowing the fudge to find its way into every corner and crevice of the kitchen; including, but not limited to, my wife's hair. She stood there watching too hysterical to scream... at first. I don't remember much after that. Things starting moving in slow motion. The dog stepped in fudge. She stepped in fudge. I tried to glue the cake back together using the fudge using my hand as a spatula.

Soon after, we were divorced. To this day, even if I see fudge in a store, I still twitch.

Forget the looks, savor the taste. There's an expression in Yiddish: Kvell... to enjoy immensely... inner pride... With this compote, the smell will make you kvell. One taste and you'll wonder why you bothered with the main course. Hide some for yourself in the back of the fridge. This is what defines comfort food!

Compote

Stove top cooking
10-12 servings

Ingredients

2 packages dried mixed fruit (11 ounce size)
1/4 pound dried apples
1/2 cup light raisins
1/2 cup sugar/Sweetener (optional)
2 sticks cinnamon (about 3" each)
1 tablespoon brandy, cognac, amaretto (optional)
6 cups water

1. Place dried fruit with cinnamon stick in a 5- quart Dutch oven or saucepan. Add 6 cups hot water to cover fruit and refrigerate covered several hours or overnight.
2. Next day, bring to boil; simmer covered until soft but not mushy (about 1/2 hr). Add sugar the last 5 minutes.
3. Remove cinnamon sticks. Refrigerate covered until well chilled or over night.

NOTE: This is a dish my grandmother always made for Hanukah. I don't really know why. It's great all year and wonderful at breakfast to get things going, if you know what I mean.

Things to buy:
• Dried mixed fruit
• Brandy, cognac or amaretto

Hamantaschen

Oven at 400°
Makes 20 pastries

Ingredients

1 package pie crust from
   refrigerator section
*12 ounces dried prune
   (dried plums) (2 cups)
3 tablespoons sugar or sweetener
3 tablespoons boiling water
1-2 tablespoons lemon juice
Cooking spray

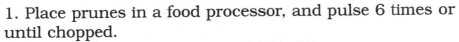

Things to buy:
• Refrigerated pie crust
• Prunes or apricots

1. Place prunes in a food processor, and pulse 6 times or
until chopped.
2. With processor on, slowly add 3 tablespoons
sugar/sweetener, water, and lemon juice through food
chute, and process until smooth, scraping sides of
processor bowl twice. Spoon the prune mixture into a
bowl; cover and chill 8 hours or overnight.
3. Unroll one of the pie crusts. Find a glass with a 3 1/2
inch round opening. Carefully stamp out 10 or 11 circles.
Repeat with the second pie crust.
4. Preheat oven to 400°.
5. Spoon 1 level tablespoon of prune mixture into the
center of each circle. With floured hands, fold dough over
filling to form a triangle, and pinch edges together to seal.
6. Place triangles 2 inches apart on baking sheets coated
with cooking spray, and bake at 400° for 10 -15 minutes
or until pastries are lightly browned.
7. Remove from pans, and cool on a wire rack.
*You can do the same with dried apricots, apples or a
mixture.

Festival Fruit Strudels

Oven 350 degrees
8 servings

Ingredients

1/2 cup sugar
1/2 cup port or other
     sweet red wine
1 tablespoon grated
   orange rind
1/3 cup fresh orange juice
2 (8-ounce) packages
   dried mixed fruit, diced
1 (3-inch) cinnamon stick
5 1/3 cups diced cooking apple (2 pounds)
1/4 cup stick margarine (1 stick)
4 teaspoons vegetable oil
1/2 cup dry breadcrumbs
1/2 teaspoon freshly grated nutmeg
16 sheets frozen phyllo dough, thawed
Cooking spray

Things to buy:
• Sweet red wine
• Orange, apples
• Mixed dried fruits
• Nutmeg
• Phyllo dough

1. Combine first 6 ingredients in a large saucepan, and bring to a boil, stirring occasionally.
2. Cover, reduce heat, and simmer fruit mixture 35 minutes or until liquid is absorbed, stirring occasionally.
3. Remove fruit mixture from heat, and stir in apple. Cool, uncovered, and discard cinnamon stick.
4. Combine the margarine and oil in a small saucepan; cook over low heat until the margarine melts, stirring well. Combine the breadcrumbs and nutmeg in a small bowl.
5. Preheat oven to 350°.
6. Place 1 phyllo sheet on a large cutting board or work surface (cover the remaining dough to keep from drying),

and lightly brush with margarine mixture. Sprinkle 1 1/2 teaspoons of the breadcrumb mixture lengthwise down the 4-inch center section of phyllo.

7. Spoon 1/3 cup of fruit mixture onto the breadcrumb mixture about 2 inches from one short end, spreading fruit mixture to form a 4 x 2-inch rectangle.

8. Fold one long side of phyllo over filling, and repeat with other long side, overlapping phyllo. Starting at short edge with filling, roll up phyllo jelly-roll fashion. (Do not roll tightly, or the strudel may split.)

9. Place strudel, seam side down, on a baking sheet coated with cooking spray. Lightly coat strudel with cooking spray.

10. Repeat procedure with the remaining phyllo, margarine mixture, breadcrumb mixture, and fruit mixture.

Bake at 350° for 30 minutes or until strudel is golden brown. Serve warm or at room temperature.

The staple dessert on the Jewish menu. Jane adds nuts and raisins... I hate nuts and raisins. Nuts give me a headache and I consider raisins geriatric grapes. But that's me! You on the other hand, will love this easy to prepare treat and your guests will swear you bought this delight at some sophisticated pastry shop. Don't modify the recipe. It'll come out perfectly. I do give you dispensation for leaving out the nuts and raisins.

I guess my dislike of raisins goes back to when I was a kid and couldn't eat chocolate; I got headaches from that too. So my mother decided that a small box of raisins (raisins have a shelf life of 30 years) is candy. Yep raisins to the left of me, raisins to the right...
All my friends enjoyed Milky Ways, Snickers, Clark Bars... Me? I was stuck with raisins that crunched like they came over on the Mayflower.

Honey Cake

Oven 325 degrees
12 servings (serving size: 1 slice)

Ingredients

Cooking spray
1 tablespoon dry breadcrumbs
1/4 cup hot water
4 teaspoons instant coffee granules
1/2 cup sugar or sweetener
2 large eggs
1/2 cup honey
3 tablespoons stick margarine,
    melted

1 3/4 cups all-purpose flour   1/4 teaspoon salt
1 teaspoon baking powder   1/2 cup chopped walnuts
1 teaspoon ground cinnamon   1/2 cup golden raisins

Things to buy:
• Walnuts
• Raisins
• Instant coffee
• Honey

1. Preheat oven to 325°.
2. Coat an 8 x 4-inch loaf pan with cooking spray, and dust with breadcrumbs; set pan aside.
3. Combine water and coffee granules, and set aside.
4. Combine sugar and eggs in a medium bowl; stir well with a whisk. Add honey and margarine; stir well.
5. Combine flour, baking powder, cinnamon, and salt.
6. Add half of flour mixture to sugar mixture; stir well.
7. Add coffee mixture; stir well.
8. Add remaining flour mixture, and stir just until flour mixture is moist.
9. Stir in walnuts and raisins.
10. Spoon cake batter into prepared loaf pan, and bake at 325° for 1 hour and 20 minutes or until a wooden pick inserted in center of cake comes out clean.

Peach or Plum Kuchen

Oven 400 & 350 degrees
8 servings

Ingredients

5 – 6 ripe peaches or Italian plums
   (I like to use both)
2 cups all-purpose flour
8 tablespoons butter/margarine
   (1 stick)
1/2 teaspoon salt
1/2 - 1 cup sugar
1 cup heavy cream, half & half or yogurt
2 eggs
Cinnamon (optional)

1. Preheat oven to 400 degrees.
2. Mix together the flour, _ cup of sugar & salt. Set aside.
3. Cut the butter/margarine into the flour mixture using your fingertips. It should feel like coarse meal.
4. Press this mixture into the bottom & sides of a deep 9 or 10 inch pie plate.
5. Put the fruit over the crust & sprinkle with 1/4-3/4 cup of sugar. This depends upon how sweet you like it. I usually use about _ cup.
6. Bake for 15 minutes until lightly brown.
7. While baking, blend together the eggs and cream/half & half or yogurt.
8. After 15 minutes, remove the kuchen & pour the egg mixture over the fruit. Sprinkle cinnamon, if desired. Reduce heat to 350 degree.
9. Return kuchen to the oven for an additional 30 minutes. The egg mixture should be set and browned.
10. Serve warm or at room temperature.

About Steve...

A native of Brooklyn, Steve grew up in the multi-ethnic neighborhood of Sheepshead Bay. This was the perfect training ground for a dialectician. As the class clown and as a very authentic sounding Chinese restaurant delivery boy, Steve learned at an early age how to use his gift for imitating accents to his advantage.

Using humor, dialects and sound effects in teaching, Steve was a real life version of Gabe Kaplan's "Welcome Back Kotter." Eventually, Steve became Assistant to the Superintendent of Schools on Long Island, New York. He also discovered he had an incredible aptitude for business and started building telecommunications systems.

He left this tremendous academic and business success behind and turned his attention to his latent love of making people laugh. As Steve puts it, "I was sick and tired of the regular pay-checks, the prestige and the educational glamour of an Administrator's life so I decided to get on the road and make 30 dollars a show." "My Mother's Italian, My Father's Jewish· & I'm in Therapy opens at The Little Schubert Theatre on 42nd Street November 3, 2006.

About Jane...

Jane was born in Manhattan and lived on Long Island for most of her life. Her mission in life: "to learn as much as I can and have fun doing it." So far, she's been an Educator (High School English), audio visual & multimedia producer, owner and creative director (Parallax Studio, Ltd.), marketing director (MBA), corporate communications director, President (The Karis Company, Inc.), adjunct professor of marketing & media (FAU), Interior redesigner (I.R.I.S.), jewelry designer, daughter (Malvina Evers), sister (Ruth Evers), mother (Seth & Arin Goldberg), almost stepmother (Vicki Solomon), grandmother (Clara, Alice & Jack Goldberg), friend (Marcia, Susan, Maida), partner (Steven), suicide prevention volunteer (RESPONSE), associate webmaster (WOW), community emergency response team member (CERT) & author *(My Mother's Italian, My Father's Jewish & I'm in Therapy COOKBOOK)*. More to come...

Visit our website at:

www.italianjewishtherapy.com